flesh & blood

flesh & blood

Photographers' Images of Their Own Families

edited by
ALICE ROSE GEORGE,
ABIGAIL HEYMAN, and ETHAN HOFFMAN

essays by
ANN BEATTIE and ANDY GRUNDBERG

PICTURE PROJECT
NEW YORK

Flesh & Blood is published by PICTURE PROJECT, INC., a not-for-profit organization that increases the public's access to high-quality photography of commitment, depth, and visual courage. For more information about our books and other projects, please contact PICTURE PROJECT, 40 West 12th Street, New York, New York 10011, fax: (212) 727-1126, telephone: (212) 255-8815.

Editorial Assistant: Meryl Levin
Design Consultant: Wendy Byrne
Production Consultant: Dana Cole
Duotone separations: Robert J. Hennessey
Color separations: Sfera, Milan, Italy
Printing and Binding: Sfera/Garzanti, Milan, Italy

An exhibition of *Flesh & Blood*, organized by The Friends of Photography, Ansel Adams Center in San Francisco, is traveling under the auspices of the American Federation of Arts. The exhibition is supported in part by a grant from the National Endowment for the Arts, a Federal agency.

ISBN: 0-9632551-0-X clothbound (trade edition)
ISBN: 0-9632551-1-8 paperbound (catalogue edition)

Library of Congress Cataloging-in-Publication Data
Flesh & blood: photographers' images of their own families
edited by Alice Rose George, Abigail Heyman, Ethan Hoffman;
essays by Ann Beattie, p. 7 and Andy Grundberg, p. 13.
"The exhibition Flesh & blood was organized by the Friends of Photography, Ansel Adams Center in San Francisco" — T.p. verso.
Includes index.
ISBN 0-9632551-0-X: $50.00
1. Families — Portraits — Exhibitions.
    I. George, Alice Rose, 1944–.   II. Heyman, Abigail.
  III. Hoffman, Ethan.   IV. Friends of Photography.
TR681.F28F54   1992
779'.26'0973074 — dc20   92-12677
                                                      CIP

front cover:
DIANA BLOK
PORTRAIT OF MY FATHER AND MOTHER, 1987

frontispiece:
LAURENCE SALZMANN
HANS AT AGE 1, 1980

TIMOTHY GREENFIELD-SANDERS

LILIANA AND ISCA, 1984

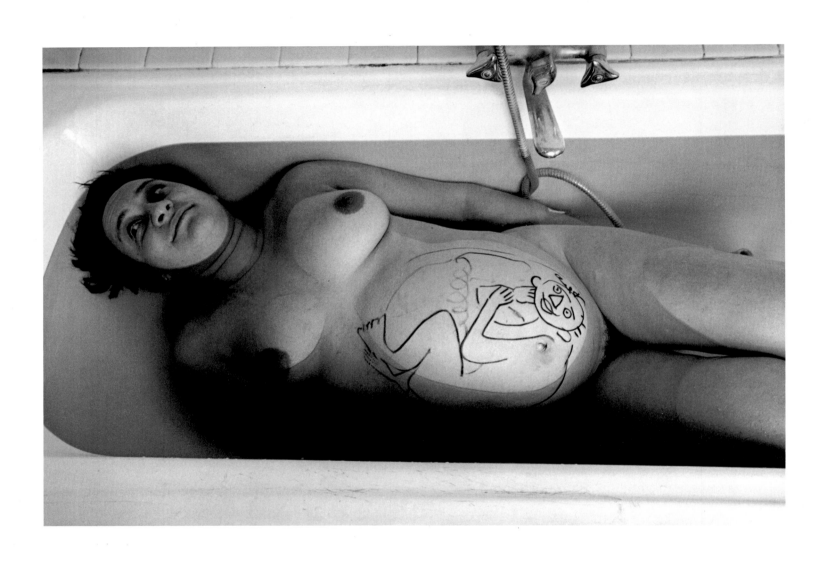

PATRICK ZACHMANN

FLORENCE AND THEO IN THE BATH, PARIS, 1986

AGREEABLE ACCOMPLICES
ANN BEATTIE

I would not have been surprised to see an anthology of contemporary poetry in which the poems were linked by the common theme of the family. But when I saw this collection of photographs, I *was* surprised: while I was familiar with the work of quite a few photographers whose images are included, I'd never really articulated to myself the obvious fact that so many photographers today are working so close to home. Because many of them have such range, and because I've been trained, in the study of literature, to look for the qualities particular to individual works, I'd failed to take an overview of the situation. Now that the obvious is apparent, I have to admit I'm a little nervous: Are families simply fair game because they can't easily run away? Would they wish, in effect, to wear Day-Glo orange vests on their autumnal walks through the living room to avoid being shot? Do parents and wives, husbands and children have a love-hate relationship with their would-be captors (after all, the family dog seems quite accepting)? Or do the subjects actually retain volition and mobility, and choose to let the photographers take their pictures out of fascination, or because of a belief in artistic entitlement, or just because they're good sports?

In some of the photographs, it's easy to imagine that the subjects were agreeable accomplices; in others, though, we are looking at young children or at infants who could have little or no say about their depiction. The photographs that I imagine to exist between those extremes are the ones I have a particular curiosity about. It's a curiosity that has more to do with process than with results, which is probably to be expected, since I'm a fiction writer. Like a lot of artists, I sidestep solving mysteries by presenting alternative mysteries. Even in the process of writing, I try to figure out how to present the underpinnings of the dress without demystifying the fabric. Through dialogue, I try to suggest what the surrounding world that constitutes the characters' environment looks like. In that world, I try to catch ambient sound as well as the way people really talk, to suggest the true tenor of what transpires; it's a way of admitting the external world so the writer doesn't seem to be constructing too neatly, or to be too conveniently excluding minor notes that provide a context for major chords. What I do — what a lot of writers do — is more about texture, touch, and sound, and with particular auditory reverberations, than might seem immediately apparent. There are times when photography seems to rely on some of the same devices as poetry and prose, while writing, in turn, so often deepens because of visual images that reverberate.

When characters talk, I want you to be able to envision their world; when they are placed in that world, I want you to be able to guess, before they speak, what they'll say. Then I hold my breath and hope things go out of control — that what was clearly in focus blurs; that something or someone begins to radiate mysteriously as my eyes blink; that I intuit — with that scary but welcome physical feeling that always accompanies switching gears when I least anticipate I might — that what I was considering close up needs to be backed away from, or that I can walk into the background because that has suddenly but certainly asserted itself as the correct site for the action. Maybe it's all an elaborate, and even perverse, way of putting myself at ease, this insistence that the picture I'm looking at, which I try to transcribe in words, has a life of its own. On a conscious level, that would take away a certain amount of responsibility, or at least would provide the illusion that dedicated viewing may result in a person or an object's revealing itself coherently. Sort of like raising the binoculars for bird-watching and seeing instead the torn fabric of a kite caught in a tree. Then, with luck, though no wind blows up to shake it free, a squirrel trembles the branch, so that the kite falls, Christo-like, over a dog standing on the lawn, and you laugh with relief because something has happened. Something unexpected, but, in retrospect, perfectly comprehensible. And furthermore, the dog is going crazy, which is every bit as interesting as seeing a bird take flight. As you are likely to tell it, the story becomes that you were looking and wisely waiting for a kite to fall on a dog's head. No kidding. It's as ordinary and unusual as that. We either say right away that we didn't expect it but were jolted into an epiphany, or we misrepresent hindsight and call it our ability to anticipate the remarkable. Other times, of course, we actually open our door and immediately see a sheathed dog, but those stories are rare, and those photographs infrequent. People who don't know how much waiting is involved when you're making art are happy to think that perfect moments, and perfect words, simply exist — then they leave it up to the artist to find them.

It seems certain that there are some photographs in this book that, if not entirely arranged, were altered for greater dramatic effect. (For example, Sally Mann's group of children gathered on the riverbank [p. 161], with one passing through what we instantly see as the birth canal.) Part of what catches our attention, I think, is the obvious presence of an adult sensibility: someone with both the distance and the experience to see the scene differently from the children.

An interesting contrast is Geoffrey Biddle's photograph of a naked child doing a dance stretch (p. 59), holding on to the edge of a table, while her grandmother, accessorized with a paper crown, looks down at something she's reading. This is a picture not about being born, but about continuing to be a child: Eve is hiding and playing, graceful and precariously balanced; her grandmother is occupied with another reality. Though her crown attests to the fact that she's willing to join in, her granddaughter has slipped away, and her attention has turned elsewhere. Most viewers will have no difficulty identifying with both people. Here, the photographer does not appear as part of the dynamic. At first, it seems to be a quickly made picture. In further study, though, what we're observing is a bit more curious: to the left hangs the alphabet, which represents what we are to learn in order to function as an adult; to the right hangs an abstract print and something indistinguishable above it (a laminated bear claw? a very bad rendition of a cactus?). The authority figure — the teacher, the queen — stands

between the two worlds. The viewer is pleased to see that for the time being, Eve has escaped both instruction and abstraction, and has been allowed to exist freely as herself.

It's interesting to find out how far people will go toward accommodating the camera. One of the earlier photographs in the book, Patrick Zachmann's view of his pregnant wife (p. 6), raises many issues. What is privacy, and what are the advantages and disadvantages of making public those things usually thought of as private? But: Can what is private really be exposed? Do we know the pregnant woman's thoughts? What will Theo think when he considers this picture years later — will it be any stranger than those hospital-taken newborn pictures we all frown at, half believing we're seeing some generic baby instead of ourselves? At first, the photograph seems strange and perhaps silly, and at the same time a little shocking. My great abilities as a fiction writer lead me to believe that the dialogue went something like this: "Would you mind getting in the bathtub and letting me take a picture of you with the baby drawn on the outside of your stomach?" However, I have trouble inventing the response. I have no trouble imagining his lines, because I see the ways in which the photographer is in control, and it's the photographer's picture. I'm not sure it's Florence's picture. It deflects too much attention to really define her; and, well, we can't believe she'll be this way much longer. (It also seems clear that it isn't the fetus's picture — it may be for him, or about him, or even to honor his existence, but, no — it isn't his picture.) Of course, I could be wrong. The dialogue could have been: "Honey, I've drawn a picture of Baby Theo on my stomach. How about taking a photo when I climb into the tub?" But I think it was Patrick Zachmann's idea — and an interesting one, because it raises so many questions and possibilities. It seems to me that it is his vision: his wife in the bathwater, his son in the amniotic fluid. And then it seems… Wait a minute: this photograph is remarkably analogous to the photographic process. Think of the way images rise to the surface when developed; that moment when, submerged in developing fluid, what was invisible suddenly brightens into being: A real thing. A picture. A Theo.

JEFF JACOBSON

GRANDFATHER AND GRANDSON, 1981

Let me back away from being struck by metaphor, though. Metaphor has most power when the thing it describes manifests itself on a literal level, as something entirely necessary and believable; only when we're convinced something is true can we discuss whether it radiates some extended meaning.

In a characteristically practical remark about writing, Flannery O'Connor, discussing one of her stories in which a character has a wooden leg, acknowledges that many people have noticed that the leg functions symbolically to represent the woodenness of her character's soul. As the writer points out, though, "If you want to say that the wooden leg is a symbol, you can say that. But it is a wooden leg first, and as a wooden leg it is absolutely necessary to the story." So, too, in photography: the components of the picture must have some difficult-to-describe inevitability about them. When they tend toward the unusual, naturally we perk up. What continues to amaze me, though, in literature and in photography, is that in the process of being recorded, certain ordinary things will seem suddenly to have an aura, even when the artist has done nothing to distinguish them by selecting a particular context. Part of the explanation is probably that in isolating anything, it becomes special, separate from the world of Everything Else. Yet I think most artists will agree that sometimes this strategy works, but more often it does not.

I would imagine it was difficult for the photographers to judge the images collected in this book. Not always difficult to make them, but to be certain that what they knew subjectively about their families and their families' worlds could be understood from an outside perspective. What would help them, though, would be the presence of the magic corona. In Donna Ferrato's picture "Fanny and Philip, Me and My Camera" (*p. 177*), that shimmering beam is presented directly to the viewer: sometimes it might have been obvious the instant the photographer looked through the lens; other times they might have had to look hard at contact sheets or prints to sense its presence. It's a curious process: sometimes it takes great effort to create a wooden leg, and other times you look up, and there it is. But whether it's made or found, it has to convincingly, inherently exist.

In my own experience, whatever I have to entirely create will inevitably not carry me one step forward. It could easily be argued that the mystical corona I hope to sense is my own happy or even desperate projection. Most artists, though, have to rely on themselves: they don't take surveys about whether something works; in many cases, they never hear any reaction to what they've created, or they get very little reaction. In order to keep going — and I don't mean to distinguish artists from train conductors here — they have to rely not just on certain knowledge, constants, and facts, but on intuition, guesswork, and what is quite often a helpful delusion that other kindred spirits will also be happy to look at the sun. It's a challenge to try to construct a wooden leg; fun to toot the horn of the train; interesting, as David Hockney (*p. 34*) has realized, to see how things turn out when you shake them and watch them settle. Photographers get to surprise people by appearing in rooms where they're not expected; they get praise from everyone but their subjects for their "candids" that reveal more than the posed photographs we all suffer through; like Joel Meyerowitz (*p. 178*), they possess the power both to create the picture and also to run in and steal the scene.

In some ways, we take it for granted that the home has become an open, public arena. Barbara Walters talks to people not in a studio, but where they live. It seems as long ago and far away as in a fairy tale that the Loud family opened the door for the cameras, and we watched in amazement as their lives transpired or deconstructed. In the not-so-distant past, it was still hotly debated whether the camera's presence created or merely chronicled the situation. These days, still photographs won't do: we want videos of our weddings. In public meetings we tell support groups as thoroughly as we can about the family life we experienced behind closed doors. We ask, either in point of fact or in effect, for information to solve the mystery of who we are. Along with professional enlightenment, or what some people mistakenly think of as the truth of the camera, we're also fond of definition by way of the senses: the way the food tasted; the song that played that summer; the color everyone was wearing. These photographs are visual equivalents of all those things. They are also *photographs*. We look at them and wonder primarily, What's going on?, in a way that we don't stop to wonder about the scent of pine in the breeze or the sound of sirens in the distance. In spite of, or even because of, the proximity to home, the people you'll see in these photographs may be closer to, or, paradoxically, farther away from, grasping certain revelations than we are. I wonder if many people would be willing to alter their own sense of self because of some work of art that decided otherwise. Or if vanity is ever easily sacrificed because someone has made a good metaphor.

By asking the questions, I suppose I'm implying that we retain what we retain in spite of images; our private world remains private, though it's perfectly fine if those private realities communicate to others in some public way. When I was sometimes tempted to invent stories, it was as much because of the photographer's presence and the process involved as it was a simple response to the content. The pictures provided me with an opportunity to understand the story the photographer wanted told. But what about the picture not taken? The larger, simultaneous picture, which naturally included the picture taker? The shadow, sometimes visible, that was projected onto the path, or onto another person's body? Far from being a missing dynamic, the sometimes quite literal shadowy form of the photographer seemed to increase suspense in all ways. The unstated rapport, or lack thereof, seemed measurable in the subject's eyes, as did his or her willingness to be there at all. Some of these images might also be considered self-portraits. Collectively, they're group portraits as well: You're sure to see yourself.

ANNIE LEIBOVITZ

MARILYN LEIBOVITZ, FEBRUARY 1979

THE SNAPSHOT COMES OF AGE
ANDY GRUNDBERG

Family pictures are the common coin of the photographic experience. They capture ceremonies small and large — first steps, lost teeth, opened presents, not to mention vacations, proms, picnics. And, given our eagerness to pose in front of the lens, they often provide their own occasion for ceremony. Once taken, these ubiquitous, palm-sized mementos are filed away in albums, dresser drawers, and wallets or displayed in carefully placed, miniature frames propped up on desks and side tables. In aggregate they constitute an inclusive, democratic portrait of who we are and what we want our lives to be. If they endure long enough, they may become the hieroglyphics of our culture — fodder for the archaeologists of the future.

The typical family photograph wears an air of self-satisfaction and celebration, fairly reeking of smiles that say "Cheese!" But family snapshots are in many ways lugubrious objects. By freezing the past, they remind us of our growing pains and rebuke us for forgetting what those fog-shrouded days were like. They present us with inescapable evidence of our own mortality, acting like electro-cardiograms of the aging process. Enshrining a moment that is no longer, these images remind us of life's losses.

Perhaps the sorriest aspect of most family photographs, though, is their thoroughly conventionalized vision of social norms. Just as in more formalized portraiture, there are rigid codes involved, but these are seldom recognized by the person behind the camera. The companies that make the cameras and films we use, however, know exactly how we take pictures: we stand eight or ten feet away from our subjects; we go outside on summer vacation but stay inside at Christmas; we hold the camera horizontally and at eye level, five to five-and-a-half feet above the ground. Little wonder, then, that your family snapshots more likely than not resemble mine.

Luckily, however, not everyone takes family photographs for granted. In the case of the photographs included here, the snapshots are interesting precisely because they constitute a genre of image that is fundamental, immediate, and unselfconscious. These non-art qualities of most family pictures paradoxically make them irresistible models for photographers who are deeply interested in extending the boundaries of what can be considered the art of photography.

If one surveys the medium's first 150 years of public existence, one finds a long and persistent effort to rationalize photography as an artistic activity and to convince the public that photographs can be art objects as much as paintings, drawings, and etchings. To accomplish this difficult task, critics dismissed the most common forms of photographic practice as being beneath consideration. Among the practices so dismissed were the broad genres of scientific, commercial, journalistic, and advertising photography; but none posed so great a threat to the notion of photography as an art than the invention of the family snapshot.

Thanks to the genius of George Eastman, whose "Kodak" in 1888 was the first successful roll-film camera, photography was transformed from an occupation to an avocation. The mysterious process that for the medium's first fifty years had been the province of skilled craftsmen and upper-class "amateurs" was suddenly a matter of aiming and pressing a button. Eastman's film- and print-processing laboratory in Rochester, New York, took care of the rest. With the Kodak, photography joined ranks with the transcendental, Whitmanesque vision of a democratic, all-inclusive art.

The popularity of the snapshot caused it to be summarily rejected by most believers in the idea of photography as an art. One of the unlikely dissenters in the campaign to distance snapshots from the art of photography was Alfred Stieglitz, the earliest and most important advocate of modern photography in the United States. Although he sought to distance amateurs from artists, he also perceived that the potentials of snapshot-style photography were vast. His own turn-of-the-century pictures — so-called candids taken at night, in snowstorms, aboard ship, and on city streets —

were feats made possible by the same technology that was making snapshot photography increasingly popular.

But if the idea of the snapshot as a legitimate style for camera artists has gradually won acceptance in the twentieth century, its most pervasive and commonplace subject has remained off-limits until recently. What makes the work of the photographers in *Flesh & Blood* so challenging is that it adopts the subject of the vernacular snapshot while still claiming its own aesthetic integrity.

Flesh & Blood is in one sense a catalogue of the ways in which family snapshots have influenced contemporary photography. These range from images that but for their forceful, Cartier-Bresson like compositional style would seem unartful to collages and montages that recycle images culled from family albums. To set their work apart, some photographers — for example, Sally Mann *(p. 156)* and Emmet Gowin *(p. 24)* — have taken to using large-format cameras mounted on tripods, giving their pictures a curious blend of offhandedness and stateliness. About half the photographers in this book have chosen to use "old-fashioned" black-and-white film, further setting off their work from the mainstream of today's snapshooting majority.

Others, like Tina Barney *(p. 36)*, Philip-Lorca diCorcia *(p. 70)*, and Larry Sultan *(p. 102)*, stay with color but intentionally blur the line between what is posed and what is spontaneous; their pictures look like simulations rather than true snapshots. Lorie Novak *(p. 108)* employs photographs projected on walls to create images within images, as a means of reflecting the enduring power of family pictures on our consciousness. The pictures of Duane Michals *(p. 166)* and Clarissa Sligh *(p. 146)*, while visually disparate, are enhanced by the texts that accompany them and amplify their meanings.

More than being merely a broad view of the styles of contemporary photography, however, *Flesh & Blood* offers conclusive evidence that family life is a crucial and unsettled subject throughout contemporary culture. The interest in depicting one's private environment and genetic heritage reflects a widespread need to understand more clearly who we are and where we come from. This is why the pictures of Jill Lynnworth *(p. 90)* and Bill Burke *(p. 56)*, among others, transgress the borders of polite convention; they use their cameras to probe deep and subtle relationships, not to affirm the already known.

Part of the impetus to turn the camera on family life is that the family unit is no longer the uncontestable, unitary model it once seemed to be. We no longer speak of broken homes, for instance, but of single-parent families. Contemporary life fills the territory of the family with such possibilities: extended families, single-gender families, second families, families of origin, nonrelational families, even (in William Wegman's *[p. 183]* pictures) pet families. In such a world, the urge to explore one's own family and to re-envision what it represents is almost inevitable.

Another reason for the current fascination with family life is that it represents a basic unit of stability in a world increasingly plagued by dislocation and atomization. In the face of simulated and virtual realities, not to mention arcane theories of chaos and deconstruction, our decentered selves can find some semblance of solace in our most essential emotional source, the preservation of our species. Overall, the pictures in *Flesh & Blood* argue for the ongoing vitality of the family as a bulwark against social alienation and emotional atrophy.

These photographs also deny the all-encompassing, universalist ethos espoused by Edward Steichen's immensely popular *The Family of Man*, the Museum of Modern Art's 1955 attempt to assay family life through photographs. Instead of claiming that human experience is essentially the same no matter where it occurs, *Flesh & Blood* acknowledges that differences exist among us and that they are rooted in the fabric of our family traditions. One of the most compelling reasons for photographing one's family is to explore the visual roots of one's genetic heritage. Given the premium now placed on cultural diversity, it is not surprising that the camera should be enlisted as a tool for discovering and preserving what makes us who we are.

Flesh & Blood is not about family snapshots, no matter how much its pictures are indebted to photography's most widespread practice; it is about the construction and inner workings of the family itself. Like much recent photography, the pictures here assert that the camera is an adept instrument not only for capturing the superficial appearance of the world, but also for revealing the significance of what underlies that veneer. If these photographs propose a rich and complex vision of family life, it is because the photographers who made them have allowed themselves to be honest with their feelings and free with their medium.

DIANA BLOK

PORTRAIT OF MY FATHER AND MOTHER, 1987

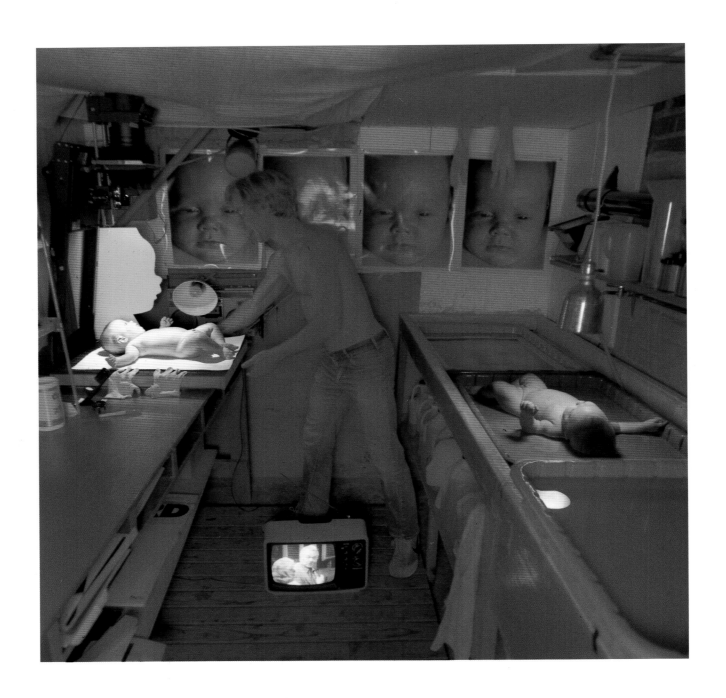

VANCE GELLERT

UNTITLED, 1983, from the series CARL VISION

EDITORS' PREFACE

In editing this book we have been moved beyond our expectations by the personal dramas that have enveloped us. Loved photographs submitted the first year would be anxiously retrieved a year later because of divorces or adolescent reluctance. The child standing stark naked at the dining table (p. 189) refused, at age twelve, to let us use this photograph of him. Now fifteen, he is allowing it, saying "I don't look like that anymore."

As editorial assistant, Meryl Levin called photographers for basic index information. She got carried away. Many of the wonderful stories in the text and in the index come from those conversations: for example, Diana Blok's description of her parents' relationship, Donna Ferrato's statement about not being married, Tony Mendoza's decision not to be a photojournalist. As we came close to press time, one photographer asked us not to publish the text she had written for us, saying to Meryl, "I'm sorry but I'm getting cold feet. I guess you didn't realize when you were doing this book that you'd become a family confidant. Thank you so much for holding my hand through this."

We like to believe that the experience of family is of happy weddings and newborn babies; it is that, yes, and more. The more makes it *more* interesting, *more* demanding, *more* emotional, and *more* connected. Family is more difficult and complex than the cheery 50's version and more loving/hating than the 80's sense of family as the root of alienation and discomfort.

These photographs are not about alienation. Neither are they "sweet," although surely many of the moments here are truly sweet. They are about people, relationships, and feelings that are very real for the photographers — even when they come from the imagination. They acknowledge the love and humor that bind the warring elements. They are rarely simple.

This project started when Abby was asked to teach a workshop: Photographing Your Own Family. Her own photographs had for several years turned almost entirely to her own family. Those images remained, for personal as well as professional reasons, her favorites. She began to see further possibilities for this subject, but she didn't think there was enough material for a major book. "How wrong I was!"

Ethan saw the potential in the idea. He taught us how to think big, seeing the idea as the book to launch the Picture Project, which was just being formed.

Alice developed an editing philosophy that gave the book a cohesive structure. She insisted that the content be focused, that the book inform the viewer with both the familiar and the novel, and that the work be contemporary — and we have almost never included photographs taken more than twenty-five years ago.

We came from three different backgrounds to form an *ad hoc* family. We pooled personal, as well as professional, experience to arrive at this selection of images. We remain angry for all the images we loved that the others didn't feel belonged, for whatever reason. We are grateful to all the photographers who submitted work, including those whose work does not appear here, for they all informed the whole.

While much of photography today is split into preoccupations with journalism, art, portraiture, conceptual imagery, and other subspecies, our selection remains eclectic.

We have defined families broadly, too: there are cousins, in-laws, grandparents, and dogs. We have not limited family to blood or legal ties because family is, in a sense, a state of mind. For example, we have included Mary Ellen Mark's and Ralph Gibson's photographs of each other (pp. 120, 121). They were lovers, and remain close friends. These are often the photographs that get dropped from the family album as years go by, as though to deny that the relationship had existed and was part of one's life. They are here.

In the middle of this editing process, Ethan Hoffman, a cofounder of the Picture Project, died in a sudden accident. He was in the heart of all that we did here. In addition to his invaluable part in coediting and codirecting this project, as Jill Lynnworth (p.90) says about her brother who died, "His memory makes my heart overflow with love. I miss him very much."

Alice Rose George and Abigail Heyman

SYLVIA PLACHY

Everything gets broken or gets lost. Worlds disappear. To photograph is to squeeze into little squares or rectangles moments salvaged from the clutter of life or from the chaos of one's family. There is no sound and there is no smell. The green juice is gone; but like the dried leaf, it's still something. It's a sign; you and they have been somewhere together.

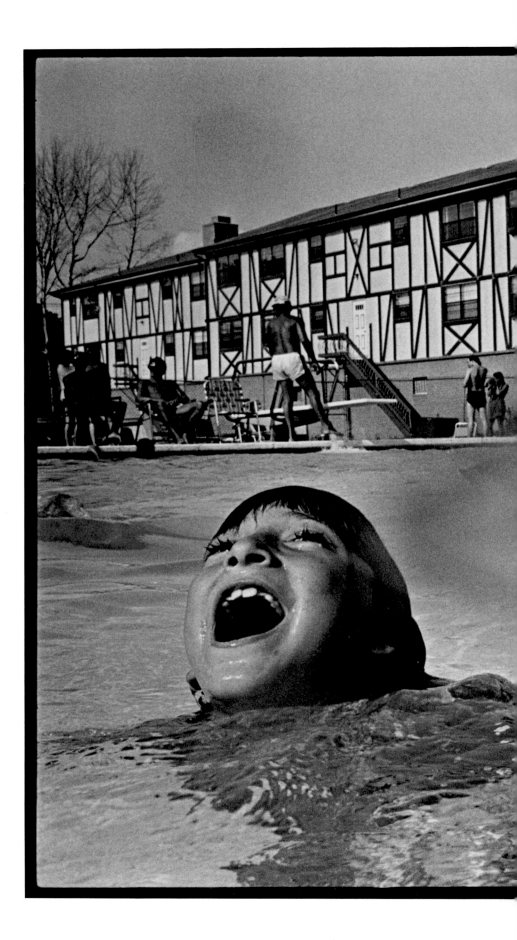

MISHA AND GRANDPA, 1980

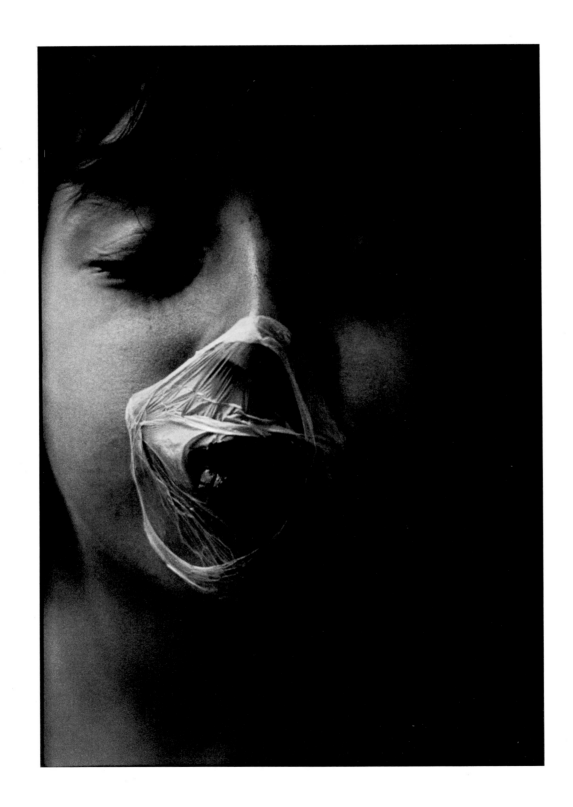

PINK VEIL, 1979

20

GRANDPA AND GRANDMA, 1979

21

ELLIOTT ERWITT

CHRISTMAS CARDS, 1959, 1977

23

EMMET GOWIN

Sometimes my photographs resemble home snapshots, which are among the richest resources of images I know. But I always want to make a picture that is more than a family record. I wouldn't say that pictures of my own family are "more personal" than the other photographs I make. But because family relationships involve some of our deepest intimacies, the photographs of one's own family do seem to burn at a different temperature.

Edith and I were born about a year and a mile apart, in the same town — Danville, Virginia. Through my marriage to Edith, I entered into a family freshly different from my own. Everything I was interested in had to do with that group of people and where they lived. I admired their simplicity and generosity, and thought of the pictures I made as agreements; I wanted to pay attention to the body and the personality that had agreed, out of love, to reveal itself.

My evolution from a single-mindedness, centered on the family and its intimate surroundings, to a larger awareness of the landscape and an acceptance of the nuclear age was a natural and necessary step for me. By backing away in physical and mental space, I could see that our family not only belonged on and was sustained by the land, but that the vegetable and biological earth had made us all. I could never again think of who we were without thinking of where we were. The physical, spiritual, and environmental shape of that whereness was as profoundly given and important to us as who our parents had been.

Just as we can never outgrow our connectedness to the family, so all art, no matter how abstract, will have its roots in the story of the unfolding of life. I also realize now that my feelings and my concerns will always hold these same people in the heart of my unconscious mind. However, as one who backs away to see the world in a greater wholeness, the visage of that dear and familiar face, the loved one, diminishes to the infinite smallness of a speck. My task — and perhaps our task collectively — laying aside appearances, is to love that indiscernible point of life as the very being of our heart's desire, as imaginatively and vividly as if it were ourselves.

NANCY, DANVILLE, VIRGINIA, 1969

RUTH AND EDITH, DANVILLE, VIRGINIA, 1966

FAMILY, DANVILLE, VIRGINIA, 1969

EDITH AND ELIJAH, DANVILLE, VIRGINIA, 1969

EDITH AND ISAAC, NEWTON, PENNSYLVANIA, 1974

EUGENE
RICHARDS

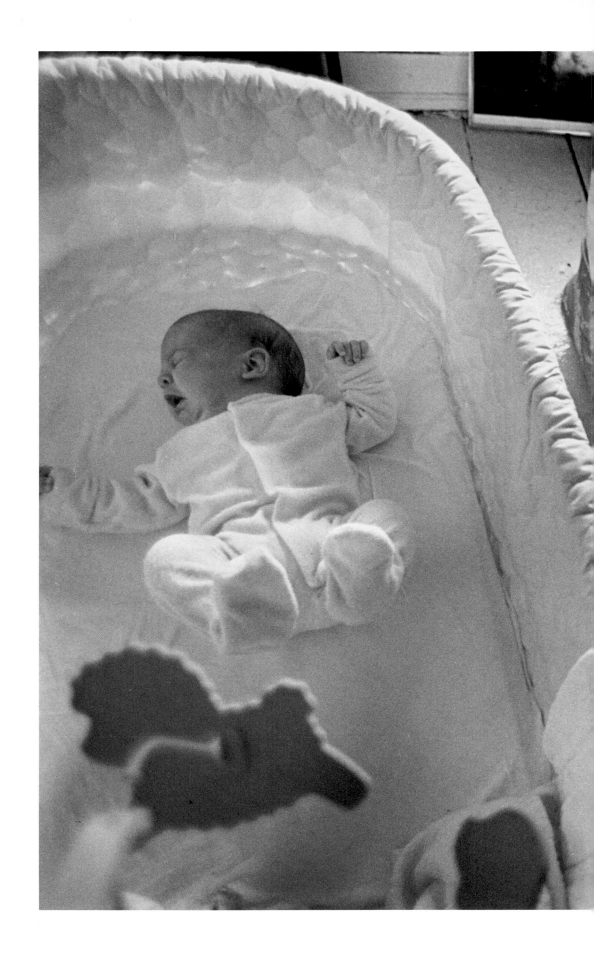

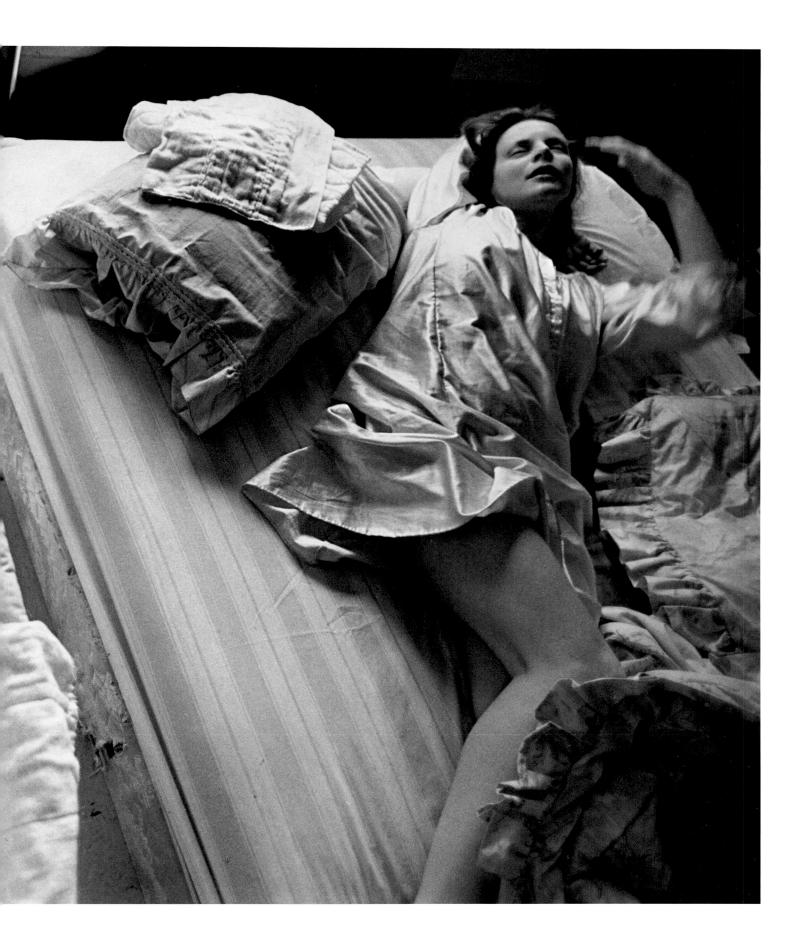

MY BROTHER, 1976

HONEYMOON MORNING, PARIS, 1982

33

DAVID
HOCKNEY

TINA BARNEY

To get a family to sit together in one place at one time is not so easy. The yearly event of taking these pictures has become a ceremony. My sister, Jill, really waits for this shoot, because it is the most one-to-one, concentrated, saturated time we might have together in the year. It's an absolutely focused time, in which I'm saying, "How do I feel about you, how do you feel about yourself, and how do you feel about me?"

The way I feel about things, and therefore photograph them, comes from the way I was brought up, how I've lived, and how I've learned to appreciate my surroundings. I question the possibility that this extraordinary way of life might cease to exist, or change drastically, because our priorities and the ways we choose to spend our time have altered so much. The time that it takes to live with quality is disappearing. I'm talking about the quality of caring — not only for the material details around us, but for our family and friends.

left, JILL AND POLLY IN THE BATHROOM, 1987

BEVERLY, JILL, AND POLLY, 1982

37

JILL AND THE TV, 1989

TIM, PHIL, AND I, 1989

39

DIANE, MARK, AND TIM AT ELENE'S, 1982

JILL AND I, 1990

41

NICHOLAS DeVORE III

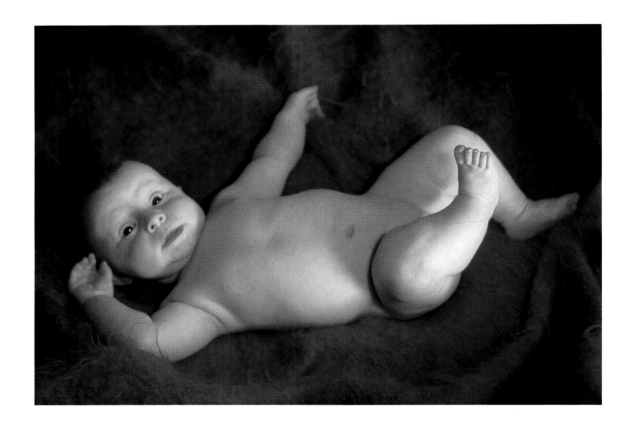

KATRINA JACQUELINE, 1988

WHERE NIKI GOT HIS RED HAIR, 1986

43

HARRY GRUYAERT

PICNIC IN BURGUNDY, 1984

CHRISTMAS IN BURGUNDY (AUXERRE), 1986

COLLEEN KENYON

I am an identical twin and have a very limited family; my blood relatives consist of mother, brother, and sister. Both my parents were only children who barely knew their fathers, and I have never known aunts, uncles, cousins, nieces, or nephews. Only as a child did I know my grandmothers. Most of my knowledge of family ties has come through snapshots in the family albums. Picturing the family is a search for authenticity, a social interaction, and, finally, a diary of perceptions. Photographing the same people over a period of years speaks of an obsession.

KATHLEEN AND COLLEEN,
WOODSTOCK, NEW YORK,
JANUARY 1979

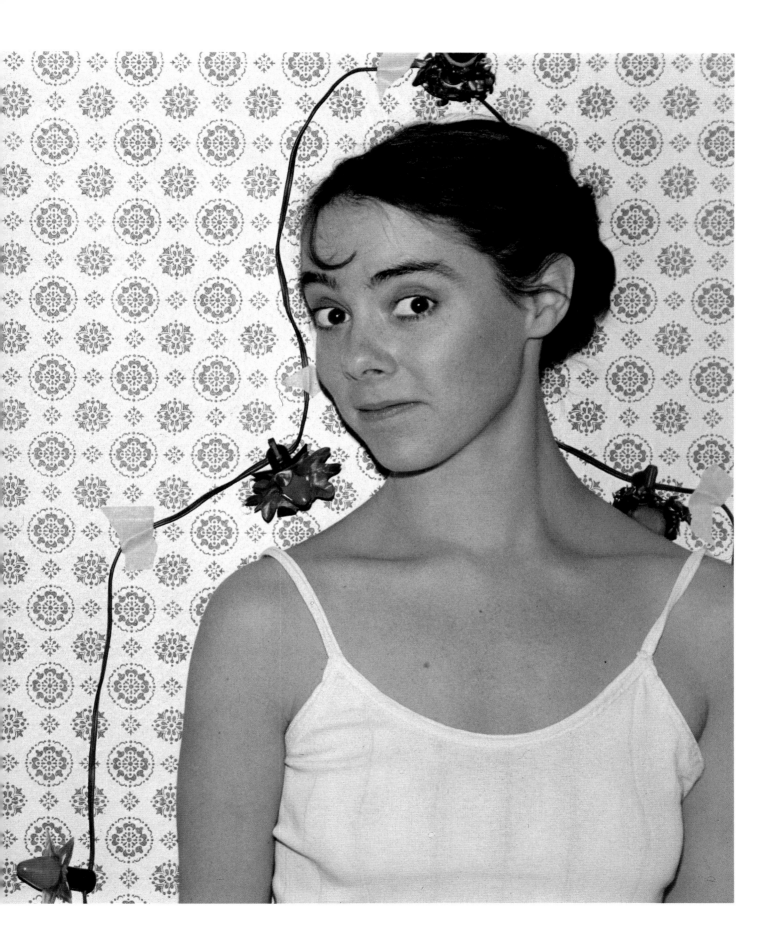

GAYLORD HERRON

JASON AND JUDY, 1974

48

JASON ON SWING, 1975

JASON WITH PORTRAIT OF DORGES, 1969

DORGES AND JASON, 1972

51

JUDY WITH
BABY KATHRYN, 1977

52

LE REPAS (THE MEAL), 1985

LE LIT (THE BED), 1985

55

CHRISTMAS, DERBY, CONNECTICUT, 1968

THANKSGIVING, MILFORD, CONNECTICUT, 1971

GEOFFREY BIDDLE

UNTITLED, NEW YORK CITY, 1986

UNTITLED, NEW YORK CITY, 1986

UNTITLED, MAINE, 1982

CHUCK FISHMAN

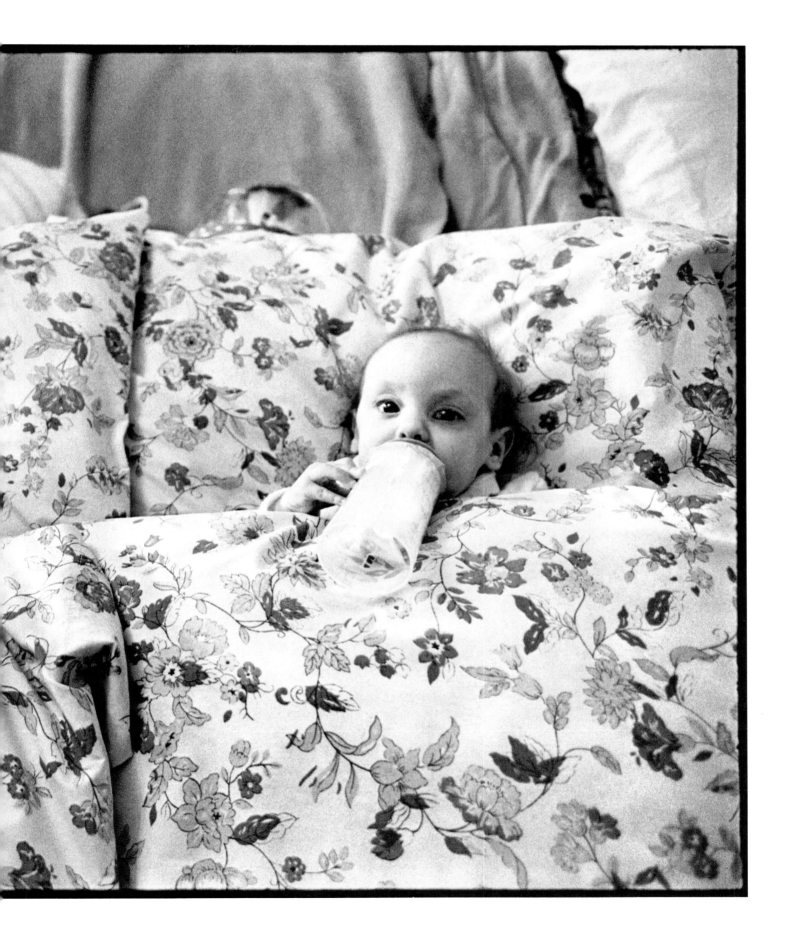

SEIICHI FURUYA

From the first day I met her, I began to photograph her regularly. Sometimes I have seen her as a woman passing by, sometimes as a model, sometimes as the woman I love, sometimes as the woman that belongs at my side. By seeing and photographing her, by looking at her in the pictures, I am finding myself. (1980)

My wife, Christine, took her life by leaping from the ninth floor of the building where we were living in Berlin-Ost. She was, for me, the closest person and also the most unknown. Photography was the best way for me to know more and more about her, and about our relationship. Since she died, I have not photographed my family. (1991)

left, SCHATTENDORF, 1981

GRAZ, 1985

65

DOUG DuBOIS

"The accident" is how my family refers to my father's fall from a commuter train in 1985. On a late-night express, he walked between two cars of the moving train and was found six hours later lying between the east- and westbound tracks. A few months after the accident, I returned home for Christmas, thinking that I could make up for what I had ignored earlier and photograph my family as before. I had not considered the distance, both in miles and in experience, that now existed between my parents and me. After dinner we usually talked, but now they stared in opposite directions, and I knew I was not in their thoughts. I sat at the table and made a photograph, but I did not recognize my mother's illness. I remained outside her grief and saw only the space that separated my parents. On New Year's Eve, my mother suffered a nervous breakdown and was hospitalized for a month.

MY FATHER, TRAIN STATION, 1984

In my most intimate photographs there is a detachment that speaks of my isolation. I no longer see my family as an assured source of comfort, but as part of the confusion of my adult life. In the conflict between intimacy and detachment, I feel the loss of my childhood family.

I sent copies of the above statement to my family. My mother answered me in a letter that directly addresses my confusion:

> Learn from what you have experienced — show your emotions, tell us what you're feeling, don't rely on your camera to do all of this for you — it won't work. Above all, search for something positive out of all of this — take hold of it and get on with it.

LISE, CHRISTMAS EVE, 1985

LISE, JANUARY, 1986

68

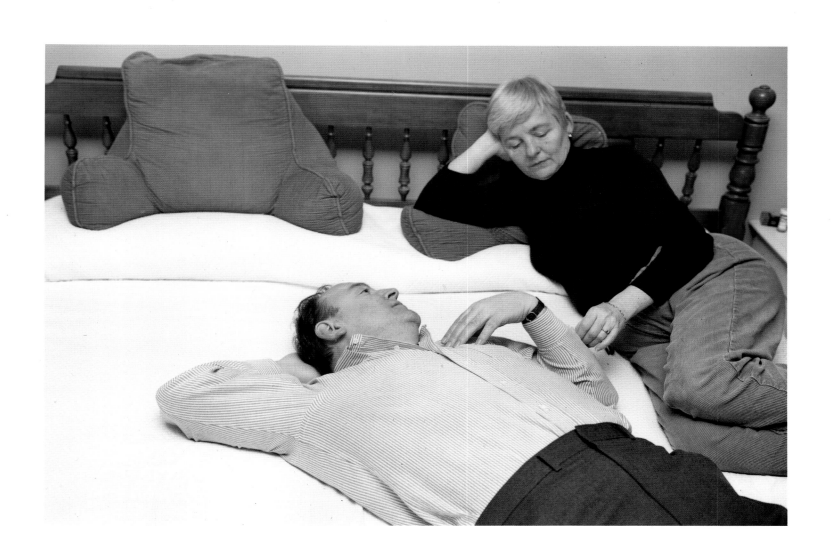

MY MOTHER AND FATHER, JANUARY, 1987

PHILIP-LORCA DiCORCIA

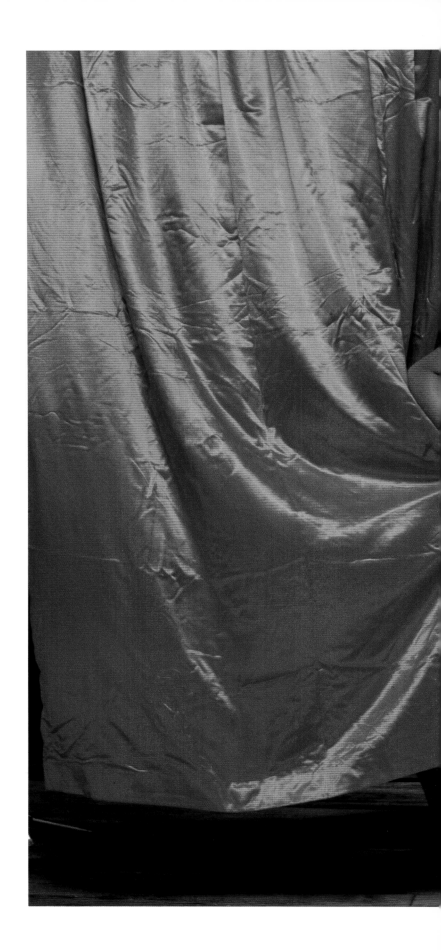

I was attracted to photographing my family both because I knew them, and could therefore say something about them, and because they were ready, willing, and able to be manipulated. At first they didn't know what was going on, but when they began to see what I was producing, they knew what to expect, and they were a lot less cooperative. As a matter of fact, I don't think I can photograph some of them now.

But I'm not trying to turn my family into characters in a little photographic novella. There are things in my pictures that I sometimes think are pathetic. Especially with my family. You know your family quite well; you know how sad they are, how certain postures indicate something about them. But some people laugh at those things that I find poignant.

Later, I lived with my brother for two years; I knew he had AIDS. At first, when his problems were still minor, I photographed him. I felt if I really wanted to make strong work that people would respond to in a visceral way, here was the golden opportunity. Once his life was threatened, I never took his picture again. I'm not willing to use my family. Yet I really wanted to. But I could never do it. I felt I would be exploiting him, although I think he would have agreed to having it done and would actually have enjoyed it.

What I do doesn't have a social purpose. If you're alive in this world and you make pictures that are sensitive to something about yourself, you are socially relevant.

MOM AND HER FRIEND, JOY, 1985

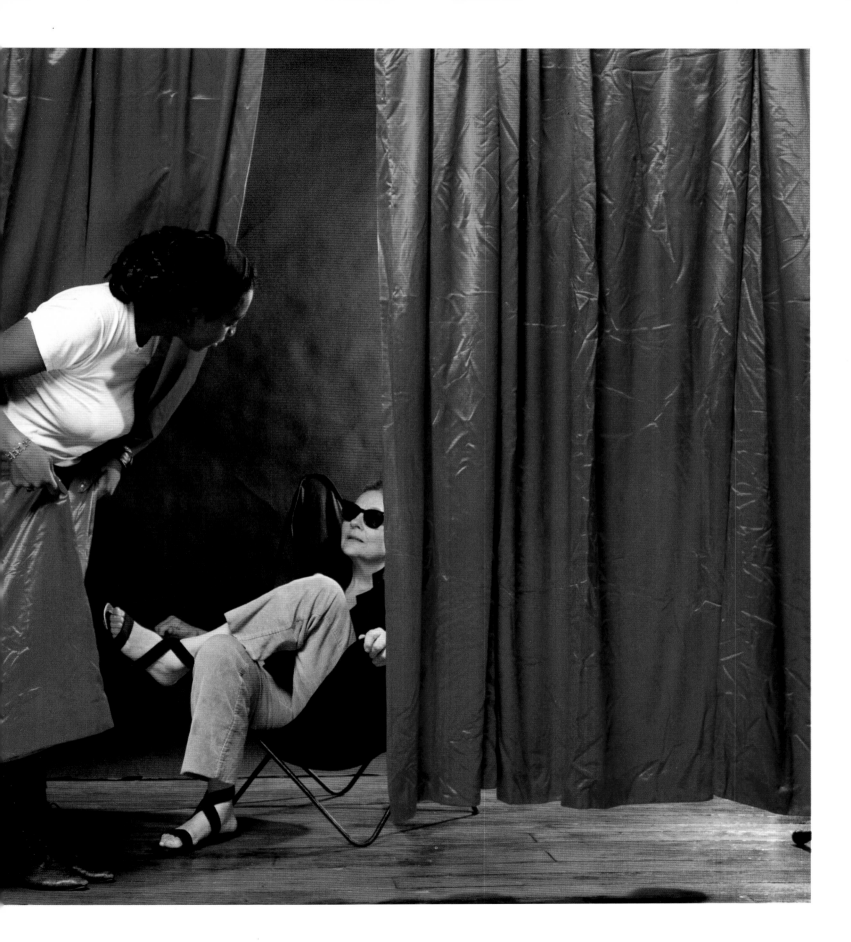

MY BROTHER, MARIO, 1979

MY BROTHER, MAX, 1984

RAYMOND
DEPARDON

top, MY BROTHER JEAN, 1958

THE ROAD TO THE FARM, 1984

top, MY PARENTS IN MY FIRST FLASH PHOTOS, 1956

MY MOTHER IN HER KITCHEN, 1982

top, MY NIECE CHRISTINE AND MY MOTHER
WATCHING OUR FIRST TELEVISION, 1967

THE FARM KITCHEN, 1988

top, MY MOTHER WITH MY BROTHER JEAN AND HIS
FRIEND, 1958

THE NEW INDUSTRIAL ZONE AROUND THE FARM, 1986

TONY MENDOZA

My grandmother, Otrin, lived very happily with my grandfather for 51 years. They met when she was sixteen. Her family had moved from Santiago to Havana, and she was being introduced to society. My grandfather asked her for a dance, and, Otrin recalls, they talked very little but she liked him. The next day, a carriage filled with orchids arrived from my grandfather; Otrin knew that they would marry. I never saw them fight.

I've always liked the idea of having a family but never felt emotionally or financially ready. When I turned 42, I started thinking that I was emotionally and financially unable to remain single.

left and above,
from the series STORIES, 1987

I went back home this summer. Hadn't seen my folks for awhile, but I'd been thinking about them, felt a need to say something about them, about us, about me and to
record something about our family, our history. I was so scared. Of what? I don't
know. But on my first night back, I was welcomed with so much love from Van and
Vera, that I thought to myself, "Girl, this is your family. Go on and get down."

It amazes me that even in the midst of a bunch of crazy, wild kids, my sisters still manage to carry on a halfway decent conversation. I mean I'm really impressed.

left and above,
from the series FAMILY PICTURES AND STORIES, 1978-1984

LARRY TOWELL

Slaves who escaped through the underground railroad planted the trees that line our farm. My neighbor stopped by to tell me that "unmarked graves of darkies was somewhere over the sand-crest in corn-goldenrod tangle." He revved the pick-up. Blackbirds scattered like buckshot in wind. — That night the moon rose like a slice of lemon, acrid on my pillow. The pitter-patter of little feet up cold stairs rough as spruce to where the shadows danced & flew away. "Daddy! Daddy! The slaves!" Heartbeat to heartbeat we synchronized. — I no longer plough that part of the field where the bones of slaves rise to the surface each spring.

NAOMI AND CAT, 1991

EATING THE PEAR, 1983

85

MARC ASNIN

Even before I began taking these pictures, Uncle Charlie was my favorite uncle. Severe depression has all but destroyed him. His wife left him and their five children; he alone has supported the children on Social Security. As I grew up, I saw him less and less. Taking these pictures made it possible for us to spend time together. My involvement in his struggle has also connected me to society's problems.

JOE AND BLACKY, 1983

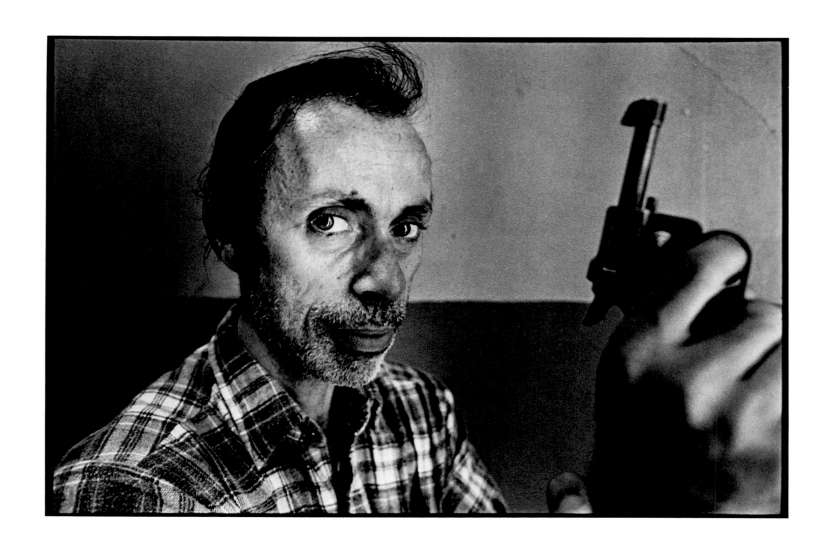

"Still there is a bitterness … what I could have been … no one knows; there was a distinct maybe."   Charlie

UNCLE CHARLIE, 1982

"These pictures will show everyone what they did to me."   Charlie

UNCLE CHARLIE AND BRIAN, 1983

"Your Uncle has one wish in life — to die."   Carol (Charlie's wife)

UNCLE CHARLIE, 1983

JILL LYNNWORTH

When I was fifteen, my thirteen-year-old brother, Randy, was diagnosed with a brain tumor. Suddenly, his life went from running cross-country and chasing girls to fighting cancer from a wheelchair. That fight lasted for five more years. The effects of his treatment drastically changed him physically, but his spirit never broke, nor his appreciation for life and sexual jokes. My own and my parents' lives revolved around caring for Randy.

Photographing the last six months of his life was my way of letting him live on. When he was alive, I didn't want to see him fading away. At first, the pictures were very clinical. I used the camera as a barrier to my seeing what was really happening to him. As I went on, I got closer and closer to what he was experiencing, and that let me do a lot of the grieving before he died. My whole family got involved with the photography, and at the funeral we passed around some of the pictures I had made. It is more painful for me to look at these pictures now. Yet I've been photographing children with cancer. In my own way, I'm trying to contribute to their immortality.

At his funeral, eight hundred people walked behind Randy's casket to the cemetery, where he could be without pain and sadness forever. His memory makes my heart overflow with love. I miss him very much.

MY BROTHER'S REQUESTED
PHOTOGRAPH, 1987

90

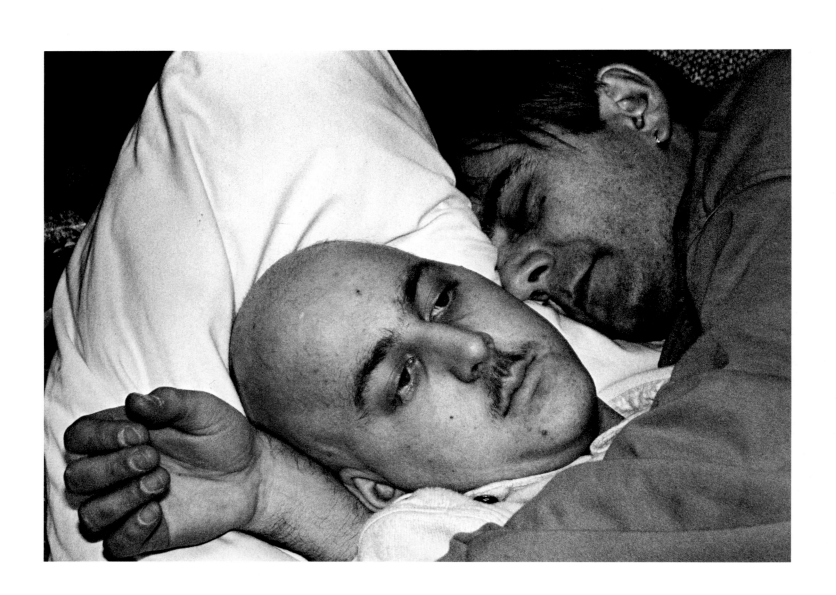

MY BROTHER AND FATHER, 1987

92

AFTER THE BATH, 1987

LAURA McPHEE

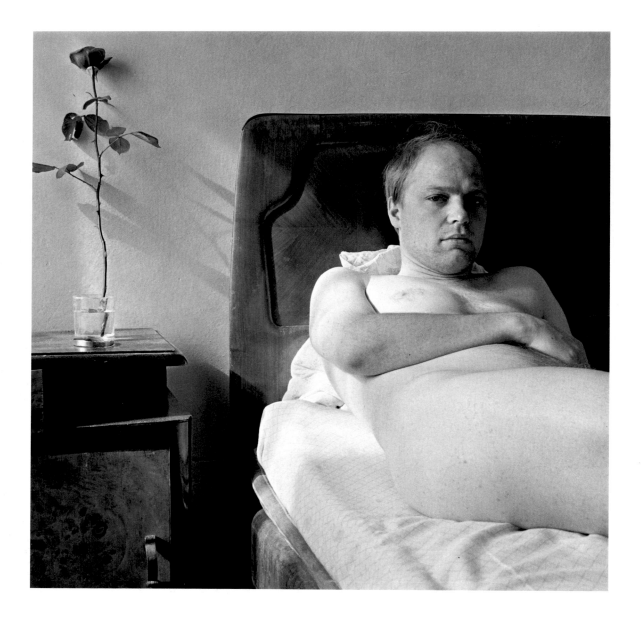

Victorian myth describes the family as a haven from the public world, as a group of people bound by birth, honor, and a common refuge. It is still prevalent in late twentieth-century American ideology, despite the reality of individual experience, which is far more complex. I am interested in the bonds that keep us actively, passionately involved with one another, regardless of the difficult, often painful aspects of commitment and knowledge. I am interested in how emotional experience can be represented physically, visually.

left, STEPHEN, PADUA, ITALY, 1987

STEPHEN AND MERLE, EASTER, 1987

95

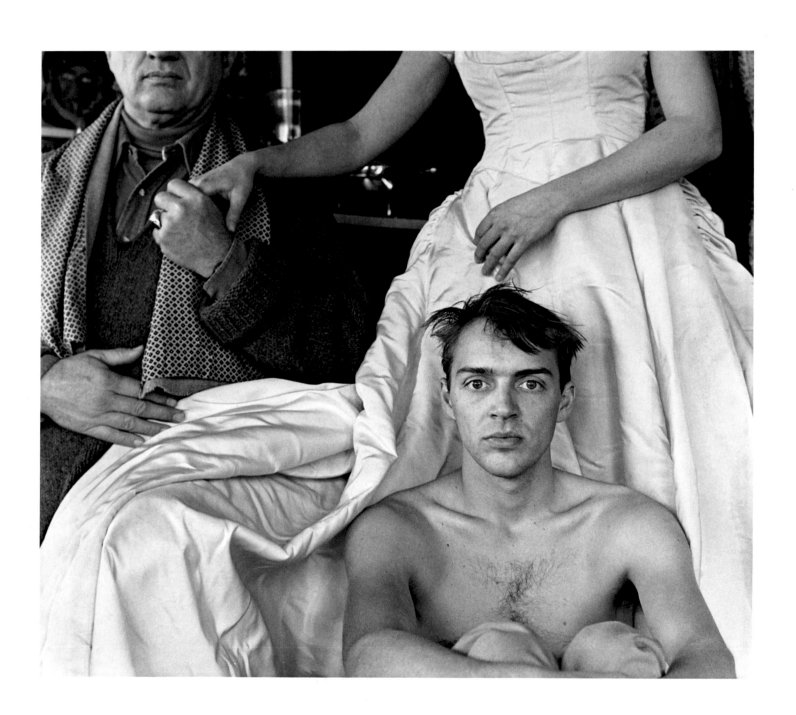

DANNY, DAN AND MARY, RINGOES, NEW JERSEY, 1987

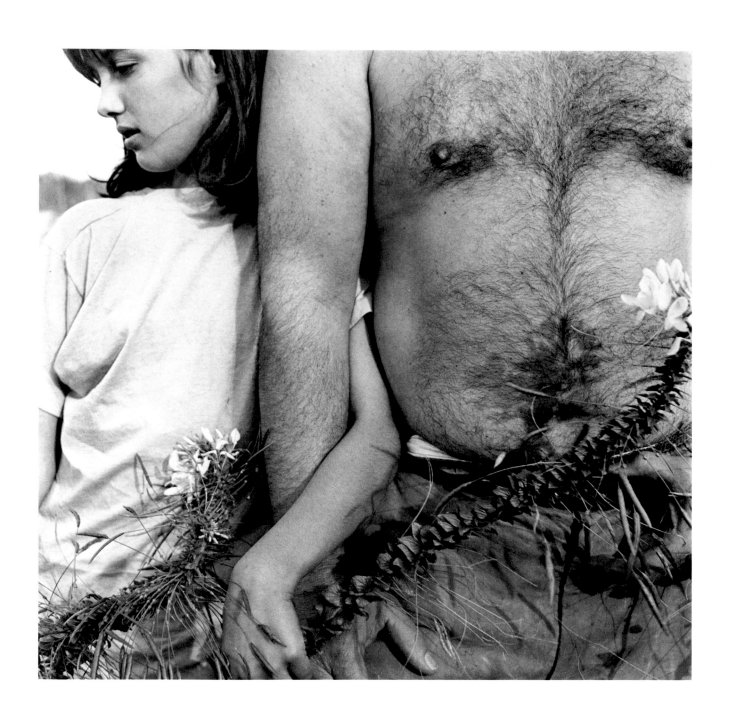

JOAN AND DAN, RINGOES, NEW JERSEY, 1986

97

CHRISTINE, VOLKMARWEG 36, GRAZ, 1981

FISH SOUP, NIBELUNGENGASSE 22, GRAZ, 1981

MY IN-LAWS, BEL AIR, MARYLAND, 1983

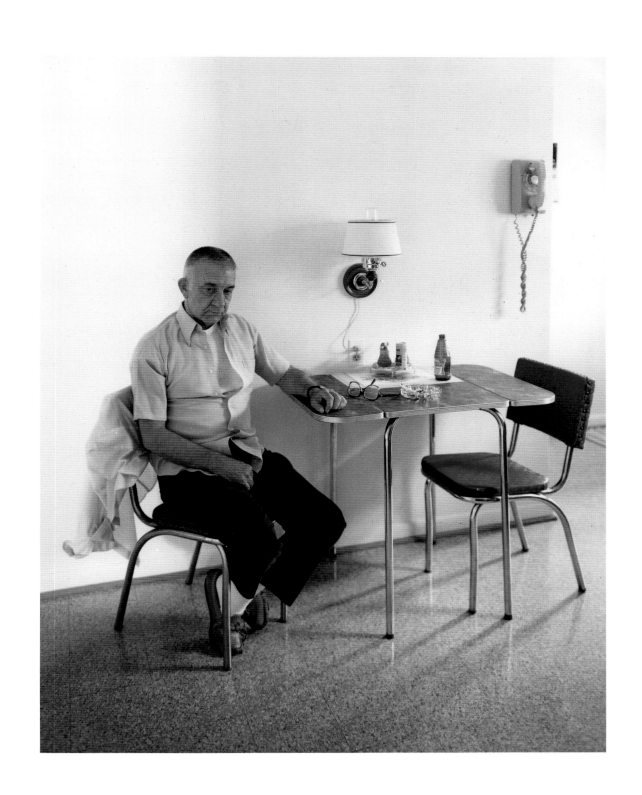

MY FATHER-IN-LAW, BEL AIR, MARYLAND, 1983

LARRY SULTAN

The house is quiet. They have gone to bed, and the electric timer has just switched off the living-room lights. As I sit here in the darkened room, it feels as if the house has settled in, sighed, and finally turned on its side to fall asleep. I'm left alone. This is the magical time when the house is mine. It is at this time, years ago, I would sneak into my mother's purse for one of her cigarettes and smoke it furiously. Now I walk through the house like a ghost searching for a resting place. I try lying on the couch, sitting in a chair at the dining-room table, looking in the refrigerator. What am I looking for? All day I've been scavenging through their house, poking around in rooms and closets, peering at their things and at them for something to photograph. I arrange my rolls of exposed film into long rows and count and recount them as if they were loot. There are twenty-eight. I can hear my mother snoring through the closed bedroom door. Without my asking, she has set a Valium out for me. It is sitting on the bathroom counter next to a full glass of water. I don't sleep well here. The pillow is too high and spongy, the sheets polyester, the blankets too thin. I wake up in the middle of the night filled with the confusion of motels. This is not my house.

———————

My father tells me, "What you do is like filming movie actors when they are standing around between scenes. But listen, it's your work. What difference does it make to me? I'm really happy to help you with your project, but if you want my honest feelings, for the most part that's not me I recognize in those pictures. All you have to do is to give me that one cue, 'Don't smile,' and zap. Nothing. That's what you get. What you call introspection looks to me like lost, empty, half dead."

———————

A few years ago I sneaked into my parents' bedroom while my mother was taking an afternoon nap. I stood by the door for several minutes to be sure she was asleep. I was so apprehensive about waking her that I adjusted my breathing to be in rhythm with hers. I had my camera, so I photographed her foot. I wanted to photograph it again and again, to use up the entire roll of film. Then it struck me that she was not really asleep, that her breathing, like mine, was fake. Just as I was secretly photographing, she was secretly awake. We were co-conspirators.

MY PARENTS' HOUSE, 1985

MY MOTHER POSING FOR ME, 1984

PRACTICING GOLF SWING, 1986

CONVERSATION ON THE BED, 1984

SUNSET, 1985

THE BARBEQUE, 1983

MY MOTHER, 1984

UNTITLED, 1987

PAST LIVES, 1987

111

W. SNYDER MacNEIL

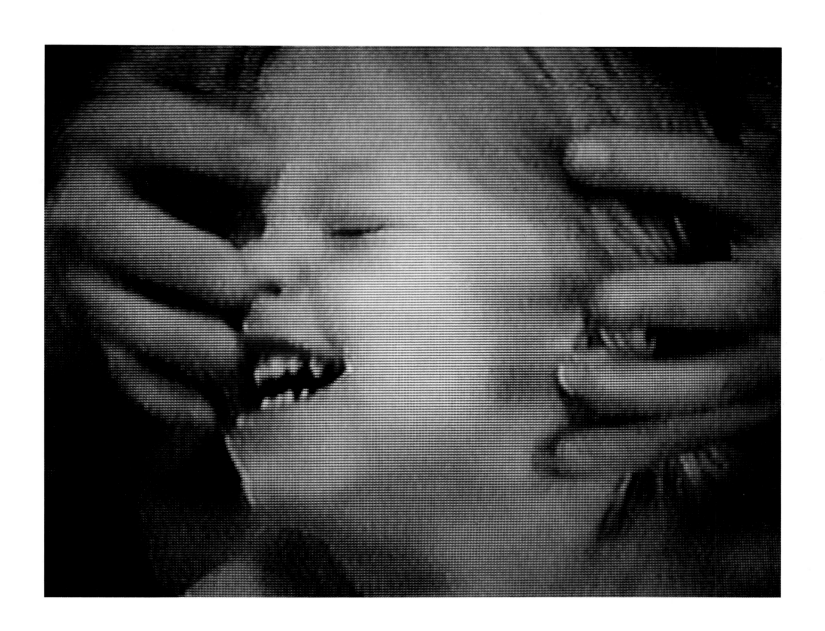

JAZIMINA AND RONALD, 1987–1989

FAMILY SNAPSHOTS, 1978–1984

PAT WARD WILLIAMS

SHE WAS ALWAYS A FLIRT, 1990
(*Mother and her girlfriends*)
from the series I REMEMBER IT WELL

ALWAYS been ª flirt.

MARY ELLEN MARK

RALPH WITH MASK, 1972

RALPH GIBSON

MARY ELLEN AT HOTEL DU CAP,
CAP D'ANTIBES, 1977

ERIC KROLL

GEORGE BERNARD SHAW DRANK MOTHER'S
MILK IN HIS COFFEE EVERY MORNING, 1985

CHARLES TRAUB

Still photography is very contemplative. The snapshooter and the professional alike are concerned with trying to hold on to the moment. Pictures of family show emotional relations that may not be expressed verbally. Everyone is too busy. Family is always immediate. They're passing right in front of us.

NEW YORK CITY, 1981

125

ETHAN HOFFMAN

MY BROTHER HOFF, WITH
SUSAN AND ELIAS, 1986

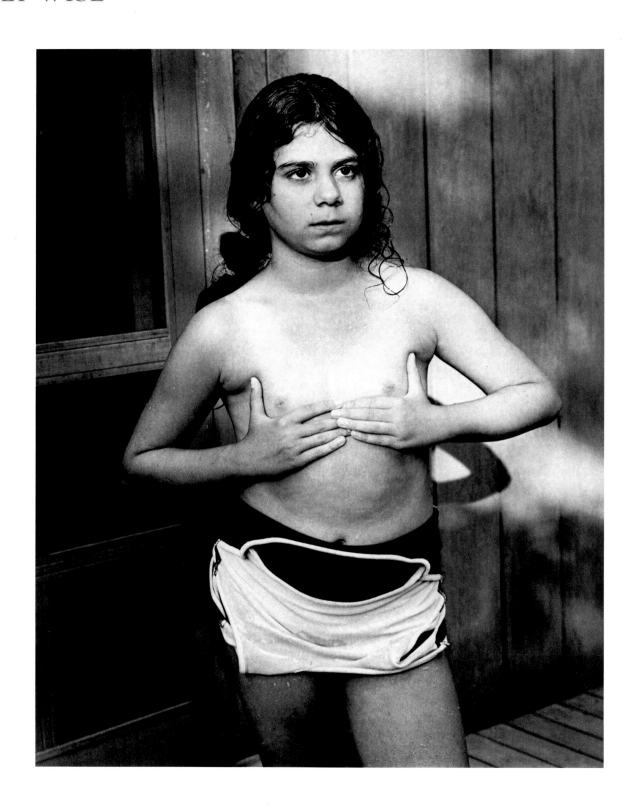

CHILD RITE, 1972

STAIRWAY, 1972

SELF-PORTRAIT, 1986

LUCINKA AT WINDOW WITH PIGEON LANDING, 1987

131

ELIJAH CLEARWATER, 1986

THE TENDER TOUCH, 1986

MOTHER AND CHILD #1, 1985

MOTHER AND CHILD #2, 1986

135

FRANÇOISE
HUGUIER

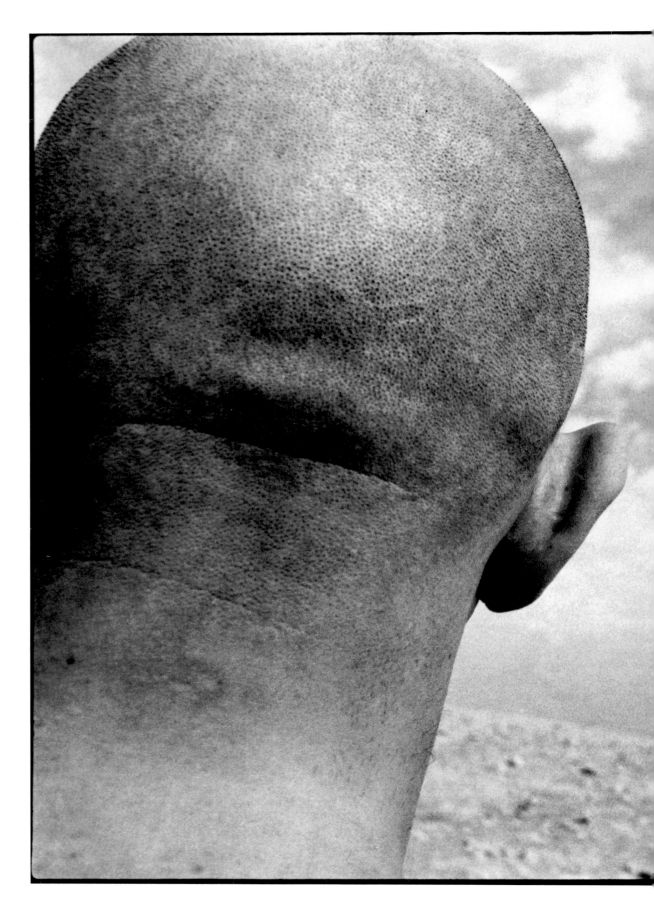

ROBYN WESSNER

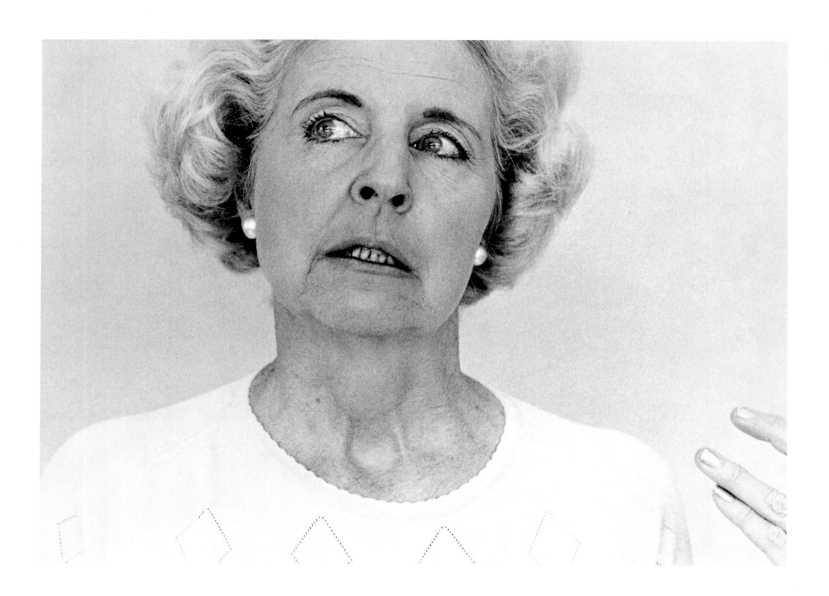

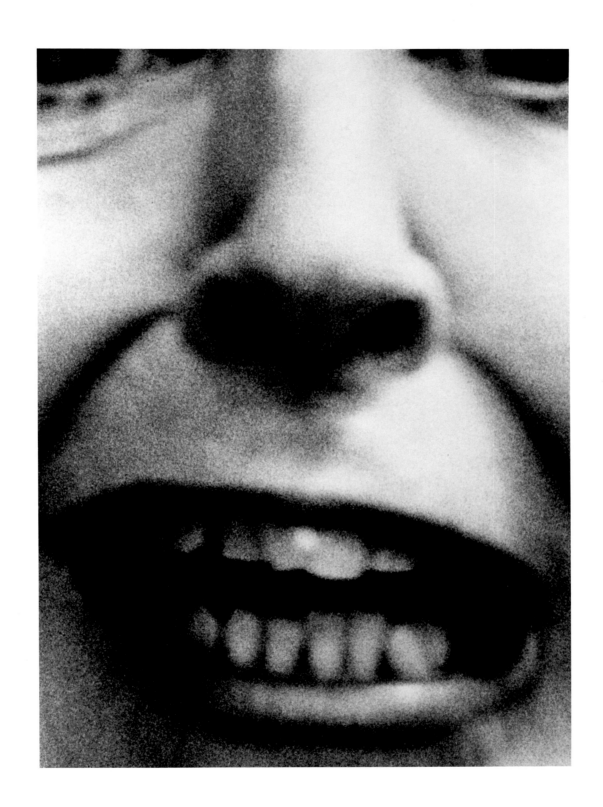

SCREAM, 1980/1982

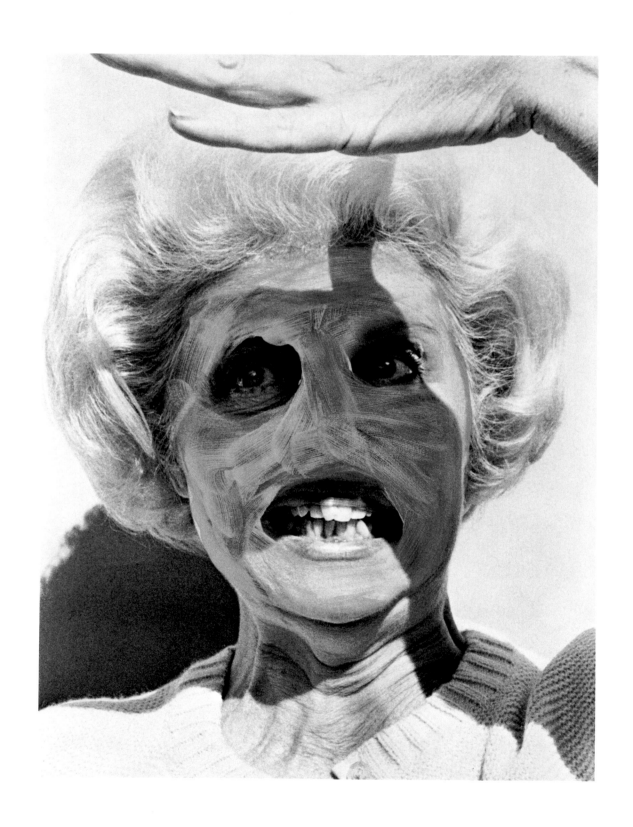

MAKE-UP, 1980/1982

140

DROPPING FIRE, 1980/1982

141

ANTONIN
KRATOCHVIL

AUNT ANA WITH PIPOS,
PRAGUE, CZECHOSLOVAKIA, 1978

142

STARR OCKENGA

My Father, Dr. Harold Ockenga, 1948

My sister, brother, and I spent our childhood summers in New Hampshire. It was the time when we were closest as a family. We left the city behind, took off our shoes, worked next to nature, and knew a "peace … which passeth all understanding." Along the porch rafters, my father set hummingbird feeders that dripped sugar water on our hair. He built us kites, taller than he was. We learned to swim, paddle a canoe, play ping-pong, croquet, and even a little golf. And we were trained in the teachings of my father's God. When the rainbows appeared touching each end of the valley, we believed that we were especially graced, that we owned the pot of gold. The next generation, our own boys, did the same.

It was the place where, by example, lesson, and spirit, we learned what our parents wanted us to know. As an evangelical minister, the pastor of a large, influential city church, and president of theological seminaries, my father loomed large for all of us. During the winter months, his

responsibilities were demanding; his time was scarce. But in the summers, he took our boys on his knee, sometimes all three at once, and was a father to another generation. Their bearing, talents, skills, and character are my father's legacy.

My father died three years ago. After he was gone, my mother often talked of how she could see my father in our boys. As a joint effort, we made a series of three portraits of the grandsons. This is one from that series. We made them at the New Hampshire house where we still felt my father's presence. Each grandson wore one of his grandfather's old dressing gowns and carried some of his sporting gear. I set up a makeshift studio in the barn he had built with my brother. The boys searched the closets, gathering my father's things. My mother helped us find what we needed. She sat on the barn stairs and encouraged us. I gave the photographs to her at Christmas. We didn't know she would die three months later.

MY SON, ROBIN, 1987

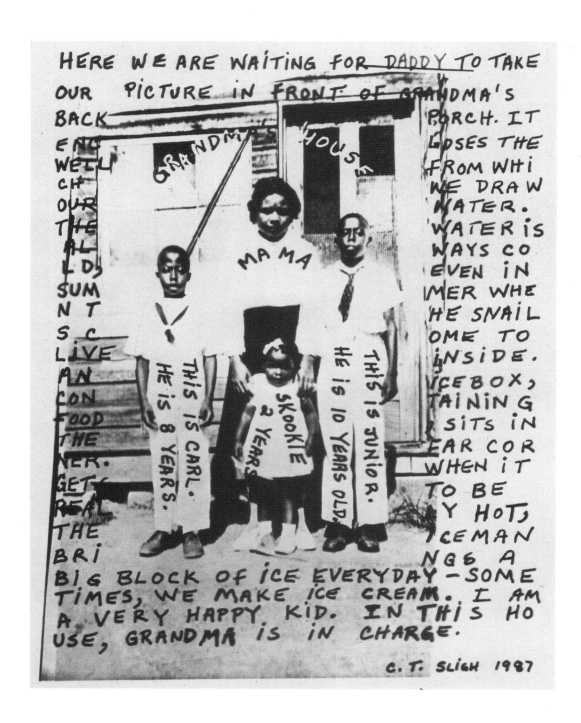

The text on the image reads:

HERE WE ARE WAITING FOR DADDY TO TAKE OUR PICTURE IN FRONT OF GRANDMA'S BACK PORCH. IT CLOSES THE WELL FROM WHICH WE DRAW WATER. WATER IS ALWAYS CO EVEN IN SUMMER WHEN THE SNAIL COME TO LIVE INSIDE. AN ICEBOX, CON TAINING FOOD SITS IN THE CORNER. GET REAL WHEN IT TO BE Y HOT, THE ICEMAN BRI NGS A BIG BLOCK OF ICE EVERYDAY — SOMETIMES, WE MAKE ICE CREAM. I AM A VERY HAPPY KID. IN THIS HOUSE, GRANDMA IS IN CHARGE.

GRANDMA'S HOUSE

MAMA

THIS IS CARL. HE IS 8 YEARS.

SKOOKIE 2 YEARS

THIS IS JUNIOR. HE is 10 YEARS OLD.

C. T. SLIGH 1987

WAITING FOR DADDY, 1987

CHERRY BLOSSOMS, 1984

147

PATT BLUE

 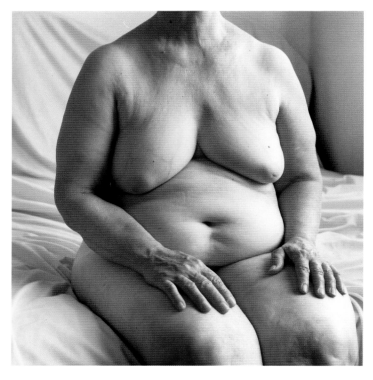

The flesh speaks so loudly in a woman's body — it fills us with secret pride one minute and burning shame the next. Generations pass not away, but into each other — breast, shoulder, hip, neck, knee, forearm, and thigh all looking backward as they pretend to go forward. I watch my mother's and my grandmother's bodies and there I am, out there in front of me; like a double exposure, it is me, but it is Mama ... Mama Eleanor, Big Mama, Mama E ... I have never been completely, undeniably sure where they end and I begin — the left breast sags a little lower than the right, the stomach is never flat, the hips spread wide. They always said, "Patricia's got the Smith hips, the Jackson behind, and Edythe's breasts ... but, really, she doesn't look like anybody in the family."

When I asked my mother if I could photograph her nude, she said, "Why, Patricia, I can't believe how much you take after your father!" She opened a drawer, reached in, and from beneath the brassieres pulled out some dog-eared photographs made by my father in the 50s. Looking as bored as she did in the photographs, she told me I could have them if I wanted them. In one she was sitting on a towel in front of a door wearing nothing else but high heels. Stoically, blankly, without apparent interest or emotion, my mother bared herself for her daughter's lens as she had once done for her husband's. As a child, I remember seeing my father do exactly as I was doing, standing exactly as I was standing, looking ... into the camera.

MYSELF, MY MOTHER, MY GRANDMOTHER, 1979/1989

My grandmother cupped one breast, thrusting it upward, illustrating where it had once firmly resided on her chest. She primly crossed her left ankle directly over the right one to relocate the swollen knee with the long thin incision line just a little beyond what she perceived to be the camera's visibility. She twisted her body, slightly stretching her torso, and thereby flattening the middle part so as to create just the right curvature of the waistline for the most flattering pictorial effects. My grandmother thought I wanted pin-ups.

RACHEL IN THE PINES, 1978

MOMS, 1979

151

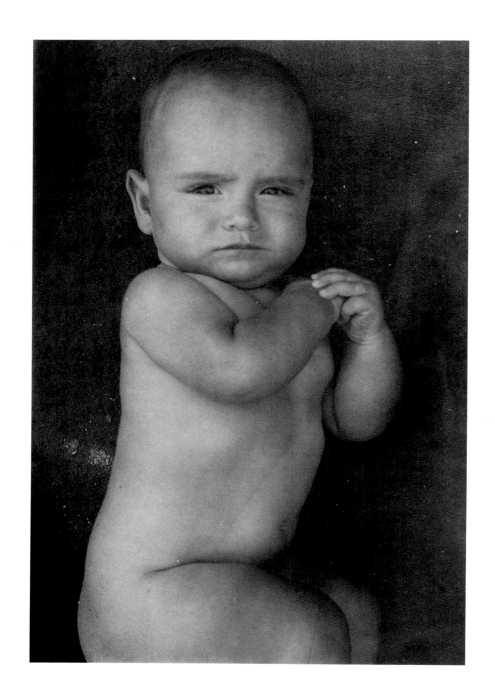

STELLA, 1978

JEFFREY, STELLA FEVER, 1978

153

STELLA, GALAXY, 1982

EVYAN, GOLDEN GIRL, 1982

SALLY MANN

Parenthood is, as the writer Wendell Berry once observed, absolutely necessary and not altogether possible — a vexing privilege and a blessed trial. I chose to have three children in five years. I have found myself disarmed by their winsome charm, as well as by their infuriating intractability. To an astonishing degree, they have expanded not only my emotional parameters but my creative ones as well.

Photographing them in those quirky, often emotionally charged moments has helped me to acknowledge and resolve some of the inherent contradictions between the image of motherhood and the reality. And it has opened up to me a world of exquisite beauty in a form and place where I least expected it.

Seeing these images is as if I were rereading old love letters. They bring on a curious surge of embarrassment, elation, and shamefaced longing.

EASTER DRESS, 1986

156

JESSIE BITES, 1985

JESSIE AND THE DEER, 1985

159

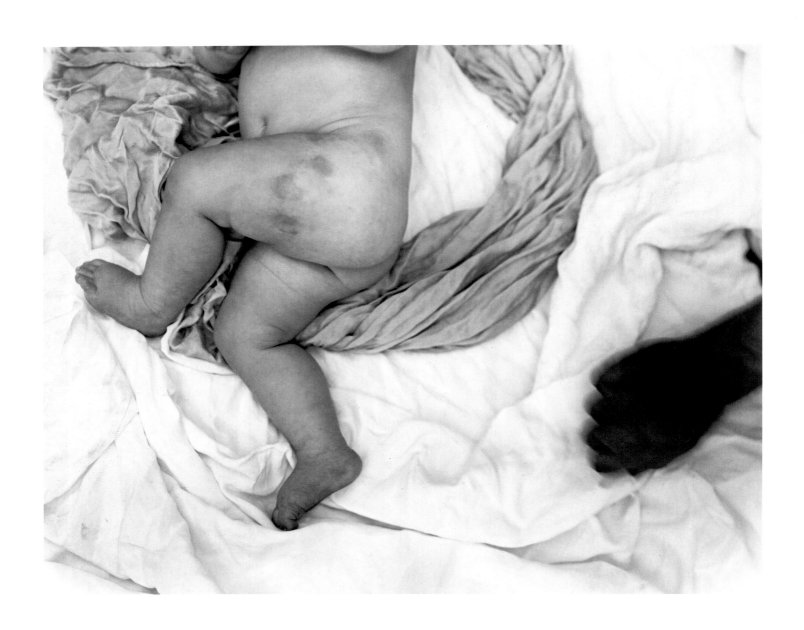

LEE'S DIRTY HAND, 1986

THE DITCH, 1987

161

MY MOTHER BEING X-RAYED AFTER HER STROKE, 1984

DEATH OF MY FATHER, 1986

163

DONALD DIETZ

FATHER, 1974

DUANE MICHALS

SHOPPING WITH MOTHER

When I was a little boy, my mother often took me shopping with her, and our last stop was always Cox's dress shop. She would set me down in a chair surrounded by our purchases and say, "Sit there. I'll be right back". And off she would vanish into the dress racks. For the first five minutes it was a relief just to be seated, but a terrible anxiety began to grow within me that she would never return. I had been abandoned! In 1932 God dropped me off on their planet and said, "Sit there, I'll be right back" Well I have sitting here now for forty six years, and the bastard hasn't returned. For all I know he's off in Andromeda trying on dresses and has forgotten all about me. And I know that he is never coming back.

SHOPPING WITH MOTHER, 1978

A LETTER FROM MY FATHER

As long as I can remember, my father always said to me that one day, he would write me a very special letter. But he never told me what the letter might be about. I used to try to guess intimacy the two of us might at last share, what mystery, what family

secret could at last be revealed. I know what I ~~told~~ wanted to read in the letter. I wanted him to tell me where he had hidden his affection. But then he died, and the letter never did arrive, And I never found the place where he had hidden his love.

A LETTER FROM MY FATHER, 1960/1975

167

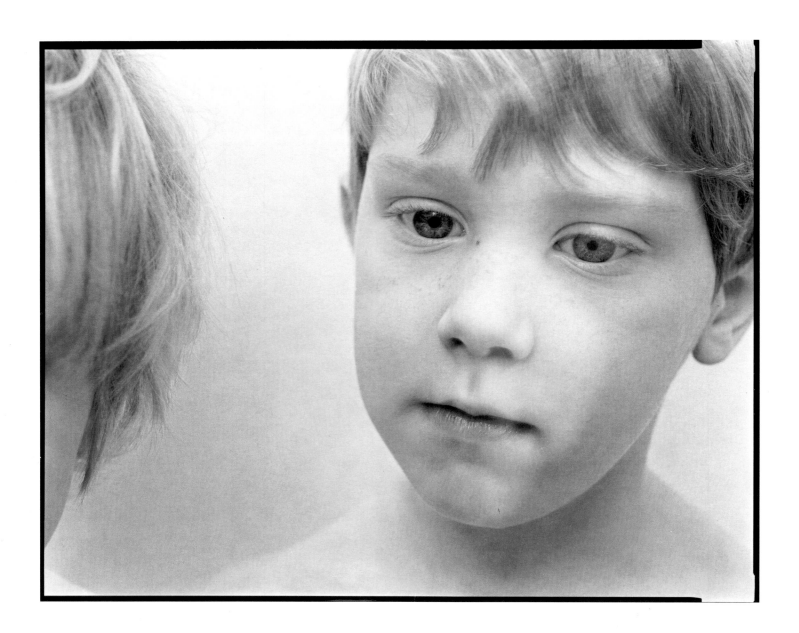

SAM, CAMBRIDGE, 1989

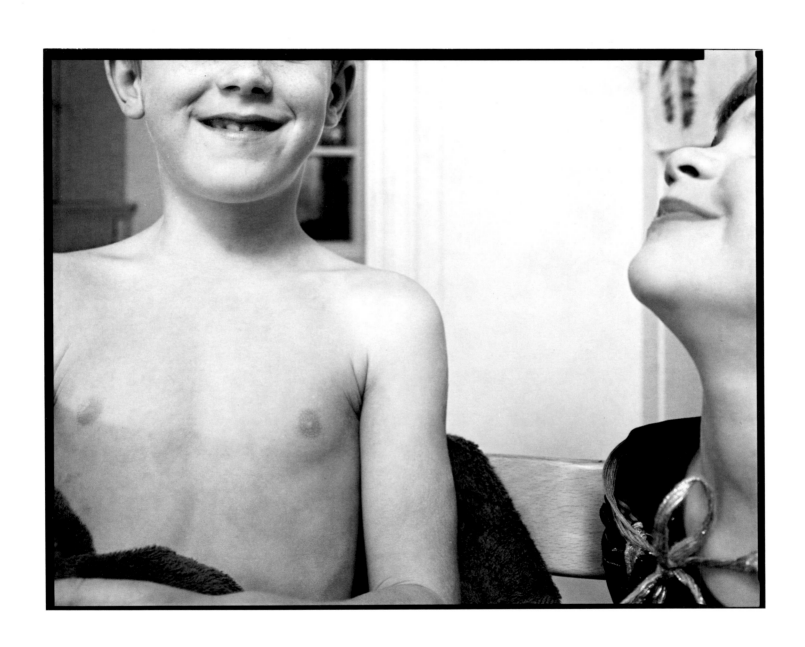

SAM AND CLEMENTINE, CAMBRIDGE, 1990

MOLLY AND JOAN, 1982

SELF-PORTRAIT WITH MOLLY, 1984

ABIGAIL HEYMAN

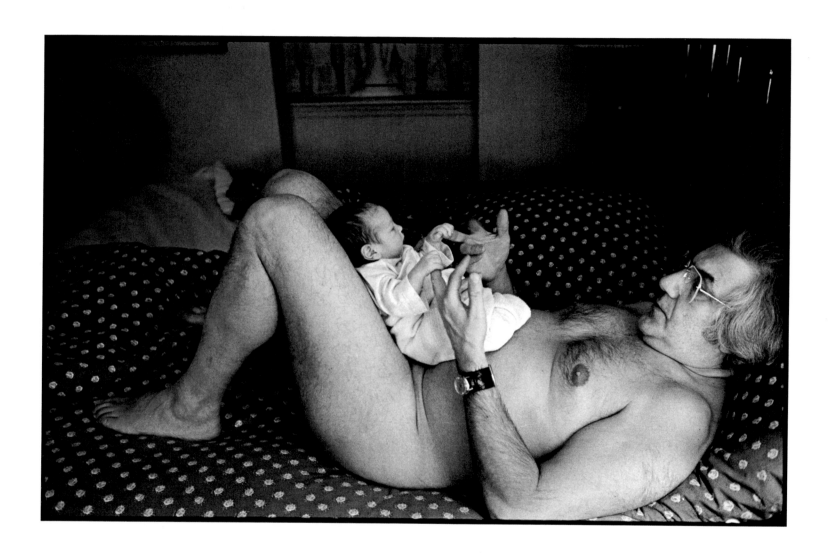

DON AND LAZAR, 1977

DON AND LAZAR, 1977

173

DON AND LAZAR VISITING ABE, 1978

DON AT ABE'S FUNERAL, 1978

175

DONNA FERRATO

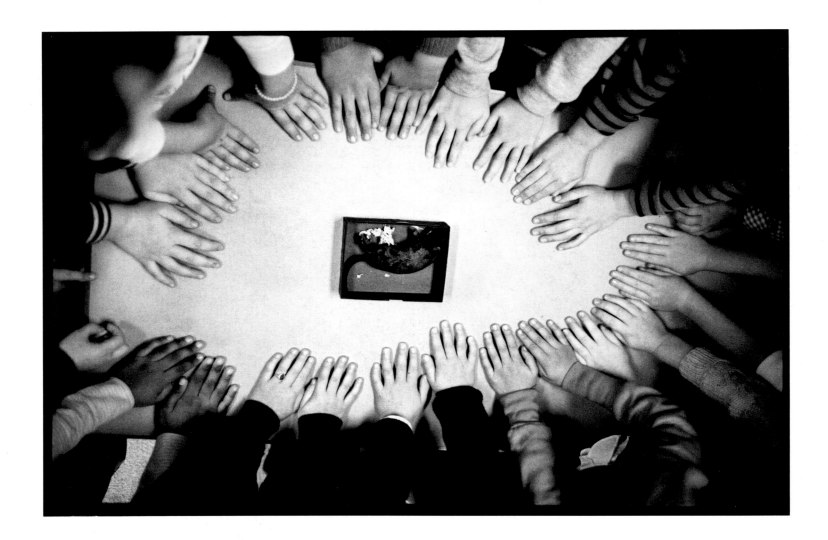

Fanny is the most important thing to me. She's made me realize the limits of time. I want to be focused and to get things done well, quickly, so I can come home and be with her. Everything I do is for her. I don't want to miss very much of her life. I do not wander now as I used to. Life is altogether different now. I am always thinking of Fanny and her children.

FANNY AND HER KINDERGARTEN CLASS MOURN
THE DEATH OF THE CLASS GERBIL, 1988

FANNY AND PHILIP, ME AND MY CAMERA, 1983

JOEL MEYEROWITZ

I am photographing my life. I have learned to relax enough to let my life be the thing I am looking at … It has taken a long time. There was a time when I didn't photograph my family. Then, one day, I was talking to Mary Frank (the sculptor), and she said, "Why do you make a distinction?" I took a step back and looked at my family and realized that they were as crazy and interesting as the rest of the world, and it changed me.

SELF-PORTRAIT WITH FAMILY, 1985

ESTHER PARADA

A small, gold-framed photograph of the wedding-anniversary celebration of my great-aunt and -uncle (March 23, 1920) is the basis of this one-hundred-frame composite. The original photograph becomes the matrix for other family photographs, dating from 1910 through 1978. My sister's face at age two, for example, is juxtaposed with her own image thirty years later and with that of a great-aunt whom we never met, although family legend has it that they were cast from the same mold. Similarly, I see other members of that family gathering through the filter of my own cumulative experience. The past is woven into the fabric of the present — genetically, psychologically, optically — and is transformed, beyond recovery.

PAST RECOVERY, 1979

MARC ASNIN's (pp. 86, 185) father was a commercial photographer; on weekends, they'd go together to take pictures of the nearby fishermen. His father taught him that the best things to photograph are the things you know the best. Having extensively photographed his Uncle Charlie, Asnin is tracking his extended family to see if its problems continue into the next generation. His work has been exhibited at the Museum of Modern Art, New York. He received both an NEA and a New York State grant in 1988. He does editorial work for major magazines and is represented by JB Pictures. He lives in Brooklyn, New York. *(American, b. 1963)*

ANTHONY BARBOZA (p. 32) began photographing under the inspiration of Roy DeCarava. An NEA grant in 1980 helped him to complete *Black Boarders* (self-published, 1980), portraits of black artists and musicians. He is working on his second book, *Piano for Days*, images of jazz musicians. He is also writing a novel with his brother Steven, pictured here. Barboza is the eldest of eight brothers. He has three daughters; he lives with his wife, Laura Carrington, an actress, and their daughter in New York City. *(American, b. 1944)*

TINA BARNEY (p. 36) was married at twenty and a mother by twenty-one. She was educated by practical, life experiences. The pictures here are in some ways directed by her, but she feels that she never asks her subjects to do anything they would not ordinarily do in their own lives. Barney has produced documentary films about the photographers Jan Groover and Horst. Her photographs are in the collections of the Museum of Modern Art, New York, and the Museum of Fine Arts, Houston, among others. She is represented by the Janet Borden Gallery in New York City. Tina Barney has two grown sons; she lives in Rhode Island. *(American, b. 1945)*

GEOFFREY BIDDLE's (p. 58) book *Alphabet City* (Univ. of California, 1992) is about the Puerto Rican community on Manhattan's Lower East Side. This work won him the 1986 Canon Photo Essayist award and a 1987 New York State grant. He works as a photojournalist for major magazines and as a commercial photographer. His work has been shown at the Museum of Modern Art and the International Center of Photography, both in New York. He lives with his wife and their daughter in Manhattan. *(American, b. 1950)*

DIANA BLOK (p. 15) says that the portrait here describes her parents' relationship: "My mother is a very dedicated Catholic. She really takes care of my father. They are very different. He was a Dutch diplomat in Argentina and the perfect diplomat, both in reality and at heart. My mother is from Argentina — very Latin and exaggerated. He is Leo; she is Aquarius. They are exact opposites." Blok has photographed in Nepal and India. Her books include *Invisible Forces* (Bert Bakker, 1983), with Marlo Broekmans, and *Blood Ties & Other Bonds* (Contact, 1990). Her photographs are in the collections of the Bibliothéque Nationale, Paris, among others. She lives in Amsterdam. *(Dutch, b. Uruguay, 1952)*

PATT BLUE's (p. 148) work is often about women as survivors. She began photographing while working for an antipoverty agency in the late 60s. Her documentary projects include a ten-year study of a family living below the poverty line. Blue's parents have been married to each other, and divorced from each other, three times. She is now working on a book that weaves her father's photographs of the family with her mother's recollections. She received an NEA grant in 1988 and a New York State fellowship in 1989. Born and raised in Kentucky and Louisiana, she now lives in New York City. *(American, b. 1943)*

BILL BURKE's (p. 56) book *I Want to Take Picture* (Nexus Press, 1987) is an innovative photojournal of war-torn Thailand, Burma, and Cambodia. He is now working on a book "about mine fields in Cambodia and mine fields at home," tentatively titled *He Only Did It to Get Out of the House*. His other books include *Bill Burke: Portraits* (Echo Press, 1987) and *They Shall Cast Out Demons* (Nexus Press, 1983). He has received a Guggenheim Fellowship (1979), a Polaroid grant to photograph ethnicity (1984), an NEA grant (1988), and Harvard's Gahan Fellowship in documentary photography (1991). He has taught at the Boston Museum School for the last twenty years. Bill Burke is divorced and lives with roommates and a dog in Massachusetts. *(American, b. 1943)*

RAYMOND DEPARDON (p. 76) cofounded the photo agency Gamma; later, he joined Magnum Photos. His books include *Chili: Special Reporter–Objectif* (with two other photographers), which won the Robert Capa Gold Medal Award; *Tchad/Tibesti* (Arfuyen, 1978); *Correspondence New Yorkaise* (Editions de L'Etoile, 1981); and *San Clemente* (Centre National de la Photographie, 1984). His documentary films include *Reporters* (1981), which received the César Award for best documentary. His feature films include *La captive du désert*, which was part of the New York Museum of Modern Art's series New Directors/ New Films in 1991. Depardon lives in Paris. *(French, b. 1942)*

NICHOLAS DeVORE III (p. 42) has been a photojournalist with *National Geographic* for eighteen years and is a member of the Explorer's Club. He is a founding member of Photographers/Aspen, a photographers' agency. DeVore was Director of Galerie FotoArte and is on the board of trustees of the Aspen Art Museum. He claims to have married "a geisha-trained Mormon." They live with their children, Niki and Katrina, in Aspen, Colorado. *(American, b. France, 1949)*

PHILIP-LORCA DiCORCIA (p. 70) writes: "When I was seven my mother left us, and I never lived with her again. There were five children in my family and my father brought us up. My older sister and a woman named Jessie were the 'mothers.'" DiCorcia moved to New York in 1982 to become a photographer. In 1986, he was included in New Photographers, a three-person show at the Museum of Modern Art. He received a Guggenheim Fellowship in 1987. It was not until 1989 that

WILLIAM WEGMAN

RAY AND MRS. LUBNER IN BED WATCHING TV, 1981

W. SNYDER MacNEIL
Untitled (My Grandmother's 82nd
Birthday), 1974

he decided to remain a photographer. He received an NEA grant in 1990. He and his wife live in Manhattan. *(American, b. 1953)*

DONALD DIETZ (p. 164) bought his first "serious" 35mm camera, a Leica 3-G, while on a European tour with the University of California Men's Glee Club. He now works all over the world as a corporate photographer, especially in the music industry. Most of his personal work involves people in urban environments. He lives with his wife, Anne Parsons, in Los Angeles. *(American, b. 1945)*

DOUG DuBOIS' (pp. 66, 186) projects both confront and distance him from family problems and involvements. He is now photographing his grandmother in a way that places his personal family history within the economic and political history of coal mining. DuBois created the photography program at New Mexico State University, where he teaches. His work is in the collections of the Museum of Modern Art, New York, and the San Francisco Museum of Modern Art. He lives in New Mexico with Elizabeth Ferran, a painter. *(American, b. 1960)*

ELLIOTT ERWITT's (pp. 22, 192) deceptively casual technique captures life's ironies with wit and poignancy. He has had one-person shows at New York's Museum of Modern Art and International Center of Photography, the Chicago Art Institute, and the Kunsthaus in Zurich, among others. His documentary films include *Beauty Knows No Pain.* Erwitt's books include *Photographs and Anti-Photographs* (New York Graphic Society, 1972), *Son of Bitch* (Viking Press, 1974), *Personal Exposures* (W. W. Norton, 1988), and *Elliott Erwitt: On the Beach* (Norton, 1991). Erwitt is a member of Magnum Photos. He has six children and lives in Manhattan. *(American, b. France, 1928)*

DONNA FERRATO (p. 176) was photographing "a wonderful family, a family that had everything," when she became witness to domestic

violence. Her continuing photographs of domestic violence resulted in *Living With the Enemy* (Aperture, 1991). She is represented by the Black Star Agency. Ferrato lives with her daughter, Fanny, in New York City. She is not married and says, "I don't believe in marriage, because I'm against the idea of property. I believe in love. Marriage is society's way of letting you into a private club. But it's a club where safety and respect and love are really not protected." *(American, b. 1949)*

LARRY FINK's (p. 170) book *Social Graces* (Aperture, 1984) is about social gatherings of both urban upper class and small-town, working class families. He is working on a book about power, titled *Brokers and Boxers*. He had a one-person show at the Museum of Modern Art, New York, in 1979. Fink has received two NEA grants (1978, 1987) and two Guggenheim Fellowships (1977, 1979). He teaches at Bard College. His daughter, Molly, lives with her mother, Joan, in Brooklyn, New York. He lives in Martins Creek, Pennsylvania. *(American, b. 1941)*

CHUCK FISHMAN (p. 62) has interviewed, photographed, and played trumpet with the oldest living jazz musicians who had played in Storyville. Several of them thought their peers had died until he brought them together again. He has done one book, *Polish Jews: The Final Chapter* (McGraw-Hill, 1977). He still goes back to Poland every few years. At the moment, Fishman devotes much of his time to fathering his young son and documenting every step. He lives with his wife and their son, Adam, in New York City. *(American, b. 1937)*

SEIICHI FURUYA (p. 64) left Japan in 1973 and moved to Vienna, where he married and had a son. He photographed his family intensely until 1985, when his wife suddenly took her life. His book of images of his own family, *Memoires* (Camera Austria, 1989), was accompanied by an exhibition that has toured throughout Europe and Japan. He works as a translator, correspondent, and exhibition coordinator as

MARC ASNIN
Jamie's Birthday Party, 1987

well as a photographer. He lives with his son, Komyo Klaus, and his mother-in-law in Graz, Austria. *(Japanese, b. 1950)*

VANCE GELLERT (p. 16) found himself a househusband when his wife was completing medical school, just after their first child was born. Feeling "trapped, bored, and hot," he began to make images that reflect his anxieties, fears, and fascinations about fatherhood. *CarlVision* (Blue Sky Press, 1987) is a collection of that work. He received an NEA grant in 1988. Gellert teaches at the Minneapolis College of Art and Design and is the cofounder of pARTs Alternative Artspace in Minneapolis. He lives with his wife, Sally Archer, an obstetrician and gynecologist, and their son, Carl, in Minneapolis. *(American, b. 1944)*

RALPH GIBSON (p. 121) studied photography in the U.S. Navy and at the San Francisco Art Institute. He completed his training as assistant to Dorothea Lange and to Robert Frank. His books include *L'Histoire de France* (Aperture, 1991) and *Apropos de Mary Jane* (Cahiers des Images, 1990). His trilogy, *Days at Sea* (1975), *Deja Vu* (1973), and *The Somnambulist* (1970), was published by Lustrum, the press that Gibson originated, which published many of the most significant and personal photography books of the 70s. He has received two grants from the NEA (1973, 1975) and a Guggenheim Fellowship (1985). He and Mary Ellen Mark, pictured here, were lovers and remain good friends. For the past fifteen years he has been happily unmarried to the fashion designer Mary Jane Marcasiano. They live in New York City. *(American, b. 1939)*

EMMET GOWIN (p. 24) says philosophically, "Nature and life gave me some good opportunities." He has taught widely and has been a major influence on recent photography. His work has been exhibited throughout the world, including a 1990 traveling retrospective that originated at the Philadelphia Museum of Art. His books include *Alfred*

Stieglitz and Myself (self-published, 1965), *Petra* (Pace/MacGill Gallery, 1986), and *Emmet Gowin: Photographs* (Philadelphia Museum of Art/Bulfinch,1990). He lives with his wife, Edith, in Newton, Pennsylvania. They have two grown children. *(American, b. 1941)*

TIMOTHY GREENFIELD-SANDERS (p. 5) studied at the American Film Institute in Los Angeles but disliked the collaborative aspect of filmmaking. He began as a still photographer by taking portraits of Hollywood stars, including the Fondas and Alfred Hitchcock; he continues to work as a portrait photographer. His work is in the collections of the Museum of Modern Art in New York and the National Portrait Gallery in Washington, D.C., among others. He and his wife live in Manhattan with their daughters, Liliana and Isca. *(American, b. 1952)*

HARRY GRUYAERT (p. 44) began working as a fashion and advertising photographer in Paris while directing films for television. He joined Magnum in 1986. His books include *Harry Gruyaert: TV Shots* (FNAC Galeries, 1984), *Maroc: Extrême Maghreb du soleil couchant* (Jeune Afrique, 1984), *Lumières blanches: Photographies de Harry Gruyaert* (Centre National de la Photographie, 1986), and *Morocco* (Schirmer Art Books, 1991). Gruyaert received the Prix Kodak de la Critique Photographique in 1976. He lives in Paris. *(Belgian, b. 1941)*

JILL HARTLEY (p. 130) photographs her daughter "to better remember her childhood, to make a souvenir of what passes so quickly." She has studied painting and anthropological filmmaking, and now works for magazines. She is completing a book of photographs from Poland. Hartley has also photographed extensively in Russia and Mexico. She and her daughter, now called Lucina, live in Paris. *(American, b. 1950)*

GAYLORD HERRON (p. 48) is a photographer, painter, and wood sculptor. He was a newspaper photographer but soon turned in a more

DOUG DuBOIS
My Cousin Sue
Marries Mark, 1991

personal direction. His self-produced book *Vagabond* (Penumbra Press, 1975), about his own experiences in the 60s generation, became a cult classic. Herron continues to photograph his family, as well as landscapes, using 16 x 20-inch paper negatives. He and his wife, Judy, have two children. They live in Tulsa, Oklahoma. *(American, b. 1942)*

ABIGAIL HEYMAN's (pp. 172, 189) book *Growing up female: a personal photo-journal* (Holt, 1974) challenges many assumptions about being a woman, from a feminist point of view. Her other books include *Butcher, Baker, Cabinetmaker* (Crowell, 1978) and *Dreams & Schemes: Love and Marriage in Modern Times* (Aperture, 1987). Heyman is cofounder and Director of the Picture Project. She lives in New York City with her husband and their son. *(American, b. 1942)*

DAVID HOCKNEY (p. 34) began using photographs as a tool in creating paintings. He is known for paintings, drawings, and theater designs as well as photographs. His photographic collages describe how we see — not all at once, but in separate glimpses that synthesize an impression of the whole. His collage here, "The Scrabble Game, Jan. 1, 1983," © David Hockney, is 39 x 58-inches. His exhibitions include a major retrospective show at the Los Angeles County Museum and the Tate Gallery in London, among other venues. His books include *Hockney on Hockney* (Thames and Hudson, 1979) and *Cameraworks* (Knopf, 1984). He lives in Los Angeles with his dogs, Stanley and Boodgie. *(British, b. 1937)*

ETHAN HOFFMAN's (p. 126) first book, *Concrete Mama: Prison Profiles from Walla Walla* (Univ. of Missouri, 1981), is a document of life inside a maximum-security prison, for which he won the World Understanding Award. He worked at newspapers in Missouri and Washington State, and later at the *New York Times Magazine*. Throughout the 80s he worked extensively in Japan. His book *Butoh: Dance of the Dark Soul* (Aperture, 1987) is about the Japanese avant-garde dance form. He was cofounder of the Picture Project, and its Co-Director until his sudden death in 1990. *(American, 1949–90)*

FRANÇOISE HUGUIER (p. 136) did the book *Sur les traces de l'Afrique Fantome* (Adriend Maeght, 1990) and is now photographing the Sammi peoples of Siberia. She had a retrospective exhibition at Rencontres Internationales de la Photographie in Arles. Huguier is represented by VU Agence de Photographes. She is married to Patrice; during her frequent travels, he often visits her for a few days when she photographs him, as in the image here. *(French, b. 1942)*

JEFF JACOBSON (pp. 9, 187) is a former civil-rights lawyer. His book, *My Fellow Americans…* (Picture Project/Univ. of New Mexico, 1991) straddles the line between art and photojournalism, using both to deal with American values. His work is published regularly in major magazines. He has received a grant from New York State (1988) and from the NEA (1990). Jacobson lives with his wife, the actress Marnie Andrews, and their son in Topanga Canyon, California. *(American, b. 1946)*

COLLEEN KENYON (p. 46) is the Executive Director of the Center for Photography in Woodstock, New York, a nonprofit artists' exhibition and education space. Her work is in the collections of the Museum of Modern Art in New York and the George Eastman House, among others. She has received grants from New York State (1979, 1989) as well as the Visiting Artist Award at the Polaroid 20 x 24 Studio (1984). She lives in Shady, New York, with her husband. *(American, b. 1951)*

ANTONIN KRATOCHVIL (p. 142) spent time as a child with his family in a "re-education" detention camp for the crime of being "bourgeois." Later, he escaped Eastern Europe. He frequently returns to his native Eastern Europe to photograph. He won the International Center of Photography's 1990 Infinity Award for Photojournalism for his work on pollution in Eastern Europe. *Work In Progress: Photographs from Eastern Europe* will be published by the Picture Project. He has one grown son, who lives in Czechoslovakia. Kratochvil lives with his wife-to-be, Gabos, in New York City. *(American, b. Czechoslovakia, 1947)*

ERIC KROLL's (p. 122) book *Sex Objects* (Addison House, 1978), portraits of American roadside sex, was received with controversy; many considered it pornography. Using his family as subjects, Kroll creates primarily erotic images. He says, "Sex doesn't end when you have a family. There are still all kinds of possibilities — all kinds of things we can work with and photograph." In 1969 he opened One Loose Eye Gallery of Photography in New Mexico; more recently, he has been working as a photojournalist. He lives with his wife and their two children in New York City. *(American, b. 1946)*

BUD LEE (p. 114) studied film at Columbia University. His first introduction to still photography was in the Army. Under a grant from the NEA (as part of the Artist in School Program), Lee worked in schools all over the country. He eventually settled in Tampa, Florida, where he founded Artists and Writers Group, a community organization for artists. Lee photographs for major American magazines. He and his wife live with their four children in Tampa. *(American, b. 1941)*

ANNIE LEIBOVITZ (p. 12) is the daughter of an Air Force colonel and one of six children. Her best known works are graphically bold and original portraits of entertainers and artists. Her traveling retrospective exhibition, *Annie Leibovitz Photographs, 1970–1990*, was organized by the International Center of Photography in New York and the National Portrait Gallery in Washington, D.C. It is accompanied by the book of the same name (HarperCollins, 1991). Her books also include *Annie Leibovitz Photographs* (Pantheon, 1983). She won a Grammy award for Album Cover of the Year (1983); for her American Express "Portraits," she won the *Ad Age* Campaign of the Decade award, as well as a Clio. She has also won the International Center of Photography's Infinity Award for Applied Photography (1989). Leibovitz lives in New York City. *(American, b. 1949)*

JILL LYNNWORTH (p. 90) graduated from the Parsons School of Design in 1989. That year, her work was included in *Life's* 150 best images of the decade. After photographing her brother, who died of cancer, she photographed other children with cancer. She is now photographing 4 x 5-inch portraits of everyone in her family tree. She lives with her fiancé, an attorney, in Portland, Oregon. *(American, b. 1967)*

W. SNYDER MacNEIL (pp. 112, 184) teaches at the Rhode Island School of Design. She has received a Guggenheim Fellowship (1973) and two NEA grants (1974, 1978). She also received a Video NEA regional grant in 1991. Her work has been exhibited at the Los Angeles County Museum of Art and the Museum of Contemporary Photography in Chicago, among others. She is represented by the Fraenkel Gallery in San Francisco. MacNeil lives with her husband and their daughter and son in Lincoln, Massachusetts. *(American, b. 1943)*

SALLY MANN's (p. 156) photographs here mostly come from her book *Immediate Family* (Aperture, 1992). She says she started taking pictures of her family because "I wanted to be a Good Mother and still remain a photographer. So I was with my children, and they became my subjects." Her other books are *Second Sight* (Godine, 1982) and *At Twelve: Portraits of Young Women* (Aperture, 1988). Mann's work is in the permanent collections of the Corcoran Gallery, Washington D.C., and the San Francisco Museum of Art, among others. She has received

JEFF JACOBSON
Thanksgiving Dinner, 1979

SYLVIA PLACHY
Gull bite (on a family
vacation), 1982

two NEA grants (1982, 1988), as well as a Guggenheim Fellowship (1987). Mann lives in Lexington, Virginia, with her husband and their three children. *(American, b. 1951)*

MARY ELLEN MARK's (p. 120) poignant photographs are often about women living on the edge. Her traveling retrospective exhibition, *Mary Ellen Mark: 25 Years*, was organized by the International Museum of Photography at George Eastman House, Rochester, New York. It is accompanied by the book of the same name, edited by Marianne Fulton (Bulfinch, 1991). Other books of Mark's work include *Passport* (Lustrum Press, 1974), *Ward 81* (Simon & Schuster, 1979), *Falkland Road* (Knopf, 1981), and *Street Wise* (reissued by Aperture, 1991). Mark has received three NEA grants (1977, 1980, 1990) and the World Press Award for an Outstanding Body of Work Throughout the Years (1988), among other awards. She and Ralph Gibson, pictured here, were lovers and remain good friends. She now lives with her husband, Martin Bell, a filmmaker, in New York City. *(American, b. 1940)*

PETER MARTENS' (p. 162) books are about people in distress. They include *1/250 on 8* (Van Abbe Museum, 1979), *Nothing Special* (Kosmos, 1984), and *Cruel Compassion* (Fragment, 1990). He has photographed often in New York City and in Calcutta. As a photojournalist, Martens is represented by the Dutch agency, Hollanse Hoogte. He lives with his girlfriend in Rotterdam. *(Dutch, b. 1937)*

LAURA McPHEE's (p. 94) mother, Pryde Brown, was a commercial photographer who photographed other people's families, capturing "the ideal manners, the happy, healthy, well-knit group." McPhee sought to expose the psychological and idiosyncratic workings of her own family. She teaches at the Massachusetts College of Art in Boston. She was a reviewer for *Views: The Journal of Photography in New England*. Her work

has been shown at the Fogg Art Museum at Harvard University and the Bowdoin College Art Museum, among others. McPhee lives alone in Cambridge, Massachusetts. *(American, b.1958)*

TONY MENDOZA (p. 80) says, "When I was starting in photography, I was robbed three times, once at knifepoint, once at gunpoint, and once at machine-gun point. I have to take some pictures now and then, but after that, I decided I would much rather take pictures of my family and pets, which is exactly what I've done." He is the author of three of the world's smallest (and cheapest!) photography books: *Ernie's Postcard Book* (Capra Press, 1989), *Stories* (Atlantic Monthly Press, 1987), and *Ernie: A Photographer's Memoir* (Capra Press, 1985). He has received three NEA grants (1981, 1986, and 1990) and a Guggenheim Fellowship (1985). He is represented by the Witkin Gallery in New York. Mendoza's wife, Carmen, was also born in Cuba. They live with their two children in Columbus, Ohio. *(American, b. Cuba 1941)*

SHEILA METZNER's (p. 152) work has evolved from commercial assignments to sensual, evocative, "unabashedly beautiful" objects. Her books, *Objects of Desire* (Clarkson N. Potter, 1986) and *Sheila Metzner Color* (Twin Palms, 1991) are collections of still lifes and portraits. Metzner is one of the few modern photographers to have her work printed by the turn-of-the-century Fresson carbon printing process. A retrospective exhibition was organized in 1991 by the International Center of Photography, in New York. Her work is included in the permanent collections of the Metropolitan Museum of Art in New York and the Museum of Fine Arts in Houston, among others. She and her husband have five children and live in New York City. *(American, b. 1939)*

JOEL MEYEROWITZ (p. 178) now works almost exclusively with an 8 x 10-inch view camera, carrying it with him everywhere he goes. The

ABIGAIL HEYMAN
Passover Seder, 1979

panorama here is printed from three such negatives. His books include *Cape Light* (New York Graphic Society, 1979), *St. Louis and The Arch* (New York Graphic Society, 1980), *Summer's Day* (Times Books, 1985), and *Redheads* (Rizzoli, 1991). He has had one-person exhibitions at the Museum of Modern Art, New York, the Museum of Fine Arts, Boston, and the St. Louis Art Museum, among others. Meyerowitz received two Guggenheim Fellowships (1971, 1978) and an NEA grant (1978). He has two grown children and lives in Manhattan. *(American, b. 1938)*

DUANE MICHALS (p. 166) began his work as a portrait photographer. He later constructed situations and created a narrative by the sequencing of his images. His images with writing on the borders are his best known. His books include *The Journey of the Spirit After Death* (Winterhouse, 1971), *Duane Michals: Photographs/Sequences/Texts, 1958–1984* (Museum of Modern Art, 1984), *Sleep and Dream* (Lustrum Press, 1984), and the retrospective of his work by Max Kozloff, *Now Becoming Then* (Twin Palms, 1991). Michals' work has been exhibited at the Museum of Modern Art, New York, and the Musée d'Art Moderne, Paris, among others. He lives in New York City. *(American, b. 1932)*

BEA NETTLES' (p. 150) work deals with autobiographical imagery. Her book *Life's Lessons: A Mother's Journal* (Inky Press, 1990) examines mother/child relationships and issues of separation, aggression, materialism, and hopes for future generations. Her other books include *Flamingo in the Dark* (Inky Press, 1979), *Breaking the Rules: A Photo Media Cookbook* (Inky Press, 1977, 1989), and *Corners: Grace and Bea Nettles* (Inky Press, 1988), her imagery combined with her mother's poetry. Nettles teaches at the University of Illinois in Urbana. She lives in Urbana with husband and their two children. *(American, b. 1946)*

NICHOLAS NIXON's (p. 168) books include *People With AIDS*, text by Bebe Nixon, (Godine, 1991), *Nicholas Nixon* (Museum of Modern Art, 1988), and *Family Pictures* (Constance Sullivan Editions/Smithsonian). He has received two NEA grants (1976, 1980), two Guggenheim Fellowships (1977, 1986), and the Englehard Award from the Institute of Contemporary Art in Boston (1985). He has had one-person exhibitions at the Corcoran Gallery of Art in Washington, D.C., and the Art Institute of Chicago, among others. He lives with his wife and two children in Cambridge, Massachusetts. *(American, b. 1947)*

LORIE NOVAK's (p. 108) photographs and installations explore memory, often using projected images of her own family. Her slide installations include *Critical Distance* and *Traces*. Her photographs are part of the collections of the Art Institute of Chicago, the Bibliothéque Nationale, Paris, and the Museum of Modern Art, New York, among others. She received an NEA grant in 1990. Novak teaches at New York University. She lives in Brooklyn, New York. *(American, b. 1954)*

STARR OCKENGA (p. 144) has taught at MIT's Creative Photography Program and at Bennington College. Her children's books include *World of Wonders* (Houghton Mifflin, 1988) and *The Ark in the Attic* (Godine, 1987). She has received grants from the NEA (1981) and from the State of Massachusetts (1983). Her work is in the collections of the Bibliothéque Nationale, Paris, and the Museum of Modern Art, New York, among others. She lives with her husband in New York City and has one son. *(American, b. 1938)*

ESTHER PARADA (p. 180) joined the Peace Corps in the 60s and taught art in Bolivia. She now teaches photography at the University of Illinois in Chicago. Since 1986, Parada has worked almost exclusively with digital technology to create photo/text or photo/collage works. She is also a critic, writing about visual representation and power. She has received two grants from the NEA (1982, 1988). Her work has been exhibited by the Museum of Modern Art in New York and the Museum of Fine Arts in Houston, among others. Esther Parada lives with her son in Oak Park, Illinois. *(American, b. 1938)*

SYLVIA PLACHY's (pp. 18, 188) announcement for her recent show, *The Danube Isn't Blue*, says, "The earth is on fire, bombs are falling, a little baby is gliding toward the flames by parachute. This was the picture my father drew as my birth announcement." She frequently visits her native Eastern Europe to photograph. She is a staff photographer for *The Village Voice*, where she has a weekly photo feature, "Sylvia Plachy's Unguided Tour." Her book *Unguided Tour* (Aperture, 1990) was accompanied by an exhibition at the Minneapolis Institute of the Arts. It traveled in Europe and Japan. Her pictures are in the collections of the Museum of Modern Art in New York and the San Francisco Museum of Modern Art, among others. She received a Guggenheim Fellowship in 1977. Plachy lives with her husband and their son in Woodhaven, New York *(American, b. Hungary, 1943)*

EUGENE RICHARDS' (p. 30) first book *Few Comforts or Surprises* (MIT, 1973), about poverty in the South, is a project that started with his work as a Vista volunteer in the Arkansas delta in the late 60s. His other books include *Dorchester Days* (Many Voices Press, 1978), *50 Hours* (Many Voices Press, 1983), *Exploding Into Life* (Aperture, 1986), *Below the Line: Living Poor in America* (Consumer's Union, 1987), and *Knife and Gun Club: Scenes from an Emergency Room*. He is a member of Magnum Photos. Richards lives with his wife and their son in Brooklyn, New York. *(American, b. 1944)*

LAURENCE SALZMANN (p. 2) has been a photographer, filmmaker, and anthropologist. His recent book, *Anyos Munchos i Buenos [Good Years and Many More]* (Photo Review, 1991) is about the contemporary Sephardic Jewish community in Turkey. Salzmann has also directed and produced a documentary film about Jewish life in Turkey. His book *The Last Jews of Radauti* (Doubleday, 1974) documents a small Romanian Jewish community. He received a Fullbright Grant (1974–76) and an International Research Exchange Grant to photograph in Romania. He lives with his wife and their child in Philadelphia. *(American, b. 1944)*

STEPHEN SHORE (p. 100) sold his first print when he was fourteen to Edward Steichen of the Museum of Modern Art in New York. He has had one-person exhibitions at the Museum of Modern Art as well as at the Art Institute of Chicago, among others. His books include *The Uncommon Places* (Aperture, 1982) and *The Gardens at Giverny* (Aperture, 1983). Shore has been the chairperson of the photography department at Bard College since 1982. He lives with his wife and their child in Tivoli, New York. *(American, b. 1947)*

CLARISSA T. SLIGH's (p. 146) diverse background includes work in the civil rights movement of the 50s and 60s, on NASA's Manned Space Flight Program, and as an analyst on Wall Street. As an artist/photographer, she photographs and uses old family snapshots to create personal and community stories and historical narratives. Her work has been included in the exhibitions *Constructed Images: New Photography* at the Studio Museum in Harlem and *Convergence* at the Photographic Resource Center in Boston. Sligh has received an NEA grant (1988) and two grants from New York State (1988, 1990). She has one daughter and lives in New York City. *(American, b. 1939)*

LARRY SULTAN's (p. 102) photographs and most of the text here are from his book *Pictures from Home* (Abrams, 1992), a compassionate portrait of his parents' affection as well as their compromises. Sultan and Mike Mandel have created the books *How to Read Music in One Evening* (self-published, 1974) and *Evidence* (self-published, 1977), photographs taken from the information files of government agencies and the aerospace industry. Both books deal with the ways in which context alters the meaning of visual images. Sultan has received three NEA grants (1976, 1980, 1986) and a Guggenheim Fellowship (1983). He and his wife live with their two sons in Greenbrae, California. *(American, b. 1946)*

ANNE TESTUT (p. 54) was a sociologist before she began to photograph. In her book *Descendance* (Mois de la Photographie/Talent, 1989), she searched for her origins by photographing her own family. She is working on two new books, *Voyages en Extrême Europe* (Editions du Rouergue) and *Les Mayas* (Editions Lunwerg). She is represented by the photo agency Rapho. Testut describes herself as nomadic; she travels through Europe in a trailer with a friend, who is also a photographer. *(French, b. 1951)*

LARRY TOWELL (p. 84) says of his first Kodak box camera, which he got at twelve, "I still like the pictures it took because they're fuzzy. The focus was set at somewhere around 20 feet to infinity and, of course, I photographed everybody closer. I still photograph my family for the very reason I began taking pictures. I love them." Towell is the author of books of poetry and photos, and an oral history. He has been associated with Magnum Photos since 1988. He also sharecrops a 75-acre farm in rural Ontario, where he lives with his wife, Ann, and their three children, Moses, Naomi, and Noah. *(Canadian, b. 1953)*

CHARLES TRAUB's (p. 124) book *Beach* (Horizon, 1977) is an intimate look at public display. He edited *Italy Observed* (Rizzoli, 1988), a collection about how photographers perceive a foreign culture. He also edited *Angler's Album* (Rizzoli), in which fishing becomes a metaphor for photography. He is now photographing for a book, *New York on the Edge*, a subjective view of New York's relation to its waterfront. He is chairman of the master in photography program at the School of Visual Arts in New York. He lives in New York City. *(American, b. 1945)*

CARRIE M. WEEMS' (p. 82) graduate work in folklore at Berkeley is apparent in the work she does today, usually about women and black culture. She has had one-person exhibitions at the Institute of Contemporary Art in Boston and the New Museum of Contemporary Art in New York, among others. A one-person exhibition of her work is being organized by the National Museum of Women in the Arts and will travel in the United States in 1993–1994. She lives alone in Oakland, California. *(American, b. 1953)*

WILLIAM WEGMAN (pp. 183, 191) is best known for his hilarious, soulful 20 x 24-inch Polaroid portraits of his Weimaraner dogs. A retrospective show, *William Wegman: Paintings, Drawings, Videotapes*, was originated by the Kunz Museum in Lucerne and has traveled to the Whitney Museum of American Art in New York and other international venues. The accompanying book was published by Abrams (1990). Wegman received an NEA grant (1982) and two Guggenheim Fellowships (1975, 1986) in photography, as well as a New York State grant (1979) in video. His work is in the collections of the Corcoran Gallery of Arts in Washington, D.C., and the Museum of Fine Art in Houston, among others. His book *Man's Best Friend* (Abrams, 1982) is about his first dog, Man Ray. He lives in New York City with his dogs Fay Ray and her daughter, Bettina. Mrs. Lubner, also pictured here, is his sister's dog. *(American, b. 1943)*

ROBYN WESSNER's (p. 138) work here uses hand-applied emulsion and painted-on developer, with color, and even makeup, applied to the photograph's surface. The images here are from a series about her mother, which also includes portraits combined with old snapshots and family movie stills. Her work often appears in publications on nontraditional photography. She teaches at MIT and Harvard and lives in Cambridge, Massachusetts, with her husband, Andrew Ruvido. *(American, b. 1949)*

PAT WARD WILLIAMS (p. 118) is best known for her installations, which integrate personal mementos with manipulated photographs, printed documents, and photocopies. Her work is primarily autobiographical, focusing on family history and black culture. She teaches at the University of California at Irvine. Williams has received grants from the Ford Foundation (1985–1987) and the National Endowment for the Arts (1990), among others. She lives with her teenage daughter in Santa Monica, California. *(American, b. 1948)*

JOHN WILLIS (p. 132) found photographing his family a natural way to join his personal life as a new father with his professional life. During the 80s, Willis photographed elderly people in a nursing home; he later returned there, with Polaroid film, to teach photography. He has taught at the Boston Museum School and at Princeton. He now teaches at Marlboro College. Willis and his wife live with their child, Elijah Clearwater, in Vermont. *(American, b. 1957)*

MANFRED WILLMANN (p. 98) founded the Forum Stadtpark, an artists' association that plays an important role in confronting Austrian audiences with contemporary art. It publishes a literary magazine as well as *Camera Austria*, a photographic magazine, of which he is editor. His books include *Black and Gold* (Camera Austria, 1981), *The World Is Beautiful* (Neue Galerie, 1983), and *The Winners* (Verlag ADVA, 1990). He lives with Christine Frisinghelli in Graz, Austria. *(Austrian, b. 1952)*

KELLY WISE's (p. 128) books include *Photofacts and Opinion* (Addison Gallery of American Art, 1981) and *City Limits* (Northeast University Press, 1987), about ethnicity in Boston. His photographs are in the collections of the Museum of Fine Arts in Boston and the National Portrait Gallery, among others. For the last ten years, Wise has been the Photography Critic for *The Boston Globe*. At Phillips Academy, Andover, he created and continues to work with the Institute for Recruitment of Teachers, an organization encouraging minority students to become secondary and college teachers. He and his wife live in Andover, Massachusetts. They have three grown children. *(American, b.1932)*

PATRICK ZACHMANN (p. 6) is a member of Magnum Photos. His book *Madonna!* (Editions de l'Etoile, 1983) is about Naples, Italy; *Enquête d'identité [Investigation of identity]* (Contrejour, 1987) is about the Jews of France. His book about the Chinese diaspora, *L'oeil du long nez [The eye of the long nose]* will be published soon. "Long nose" is a phrase used by Asians to refer to Europeans. Zachmann won the Prix Niepce in 1989. He lives in Paris with his wife, Florence, and their son, Theo. *(French, b. 1955)*

WILLIAM WEGMAN,
Mother's Day, 1989

Above all, we thank the photographers who have been willing to share their lives, and we thank their families who have participated, whether directly within the photographs, or indirectly in supporting the creative process.

Our special thanks to Peter Howe, whose initial and generous belief in this book made its publication possible. For brains, courage and heart, we thank several wizards: Nubar Alexanian, Robert Kirschenbaum, Robert Pledge, and Julia Scully.

For both practical solutions and inventive advice we are grateful to Sheldon Fogelman, Betsy Gammons, Jeanne Hedstrom, and Charles Melcher. In early phases of design, Janice Braverman, Margery Peters, and Mary Petruska were invaluable; Nan Jernigan and Nancy Robbins were essential in the plans for production.

For their enthusiasm in seeking out photographs — beyond the call of professional duty — we thank Janet Bordon, New York; Christian Caujolle at VU, Paris; Vernice Klier at Rapho, Paris; Elizabeth Krist, New York; Fabienne Muddu at Magnum, Paris; and Mark Sealy at Network, London. Our thanks to editorial interns, on whom, as a non-profit organization, we depend: Christine Butler, Joann Coates, Tim Donehoo, Sharyn Hurwitz, Jennifer Lee, Carmel Zucker.

This book is dedicated — with love —
to our own families, and especially to
Louise Fairman and James George,
Don Bloch and Lazar Heyman-Bloch,
and Ann, Karen, and Robert Hoffman.

ELLIOTT ERWITT
East Hampton,
New York, 1981